Women and perestroika

This book is published with the aid of the Bookmarks Publishing Co-operative. Many socialists have some savings put aside, probably in a bank or savings bank. While it is there, this money is being loaned out by the bank to some business or other to further the capitalist search for profit. We believe it is better loaned to a socialist venture to further the struggle for socialism. That's how the co-operative works: in return for a loan, repayable at a month's notice, members receive free copies of books published by Boookmarks. At the time this book was published, the co-operative had more than 300 members, from as far apart as London and Malaysia, Canada and Norway.
Like to know more? Write to the Bookmarks Publishing Co-operative, 265 Seven Sisters Road, Finsbury Park, London N4 2DE, England.

Bookmarks
London, Chicago and Melbourne

Women and perestroika

Chanie Rosenberg

Women and perestroika / *Chanie Rosenberg*
First published October 1989.
Bookmarks, 265 Seven Sisters Road, London N4 2DE, England
Bookmarks, PO Box 16085, Chicago, IL 60616, USA
Bookmarks, GPO Box 1473N, Melbourne 3001, Australia
Copyright © Bookmarks and Chanie Rosenberg

ISBN 0 906224 53 5

Printed by Cox and Wyman Limited, Reading, England
Cover design by Roger Huddle

Contents

Introduction / *7*

Part one: Women in Russia today
    1: Women and work / *15*
    2: Housing / *21*
    3: Consumer goods / *30*
    4: Health / *38*
    5: The family / *47*
    6: Prostitution / *56*
    7: By what road? / *63*

Part two: From the Tsar to perestroika
    1: Women under Tsarism / *67*
    2: Liberation through revolution / *74*
    3: Stalinism / *84*
    4: What does perestroika offer? / *96*

Notes / *113*
Index / *125*

Acknowledgements
The original draft of this work was an effusion of excitement generated by the revelations of *glasnost*. This needed whipping into a shape that made sense of the disclosures, uncovering their causes and explaining their background. This task was greatly assisted by Alex Callinicos, Tony Cliff, Lindsey German and Donny Gluckstein. It was most particularly helped on by suggestions from Peter Marsden, who spent much time on editorial *perestroika* (restructuring). I thank them all.
Chanie Rosenberg, London, September 1989

Chanie Rosenberg is a member of the Socialist Workers Party in Britain. A former teacher, she is the author of the pamphlets **Education and Society** (1974) and **Education and Revolution** (1975), and one previous book, **1919: Britain on the brink of revolution** (Bookmarks 1987).

Introduction

Anyone who knows anything of history knows that great social changes are impossible without the feminine ferment. Social progress can be measured exactly by the social position of the fair sex.
—*Karl Marx, letter to Dr Kugelmann, 12 December 1868*

FEMINISTS, including socialist feminists, proclaim that the achievement of socialism does not signify the achievement of women's liberation. As proof they point to Russia, which they call socialist but where women are far from equal or liberated. Hilda Scott in **Women and Socialism** says: '...socialism has not yet succeeded in making women free and equal... most women in socialist countries are not realising their potentialities.'[1] This argument strengthens the more basic tenet that women's oppression is rooted not in class society but in relations between men and women which are patriarchal. Mary Buckley in **Soviet Sisterhood** says of 'the position of women in socialist systems... So long as the majority of the top Soviet leaders are male, it seems that the woman question will remain subordinate to economic, demographic and patriarchal imperatives.'[2]

The core of the argument of this book is that women have not achieved liberation in Russia, *because socialism has not been achieved there.*

The founders of revolutionary socialism recognised the position of women in society as a measure of social progress or regress, as is evidenced by Marx's statement quoted above. Lenin spoke in similar terms. Trotsky repeated this, saying that it is 'possible to evaluate a human society by the attitude it has toward woman, toward the mother and toward the child.'[3] And not only evaluate it: 'In order to change the conditions of life we must learn to see them through the eyes of women,' wrote Trotsky.[4]

This is profoundly true. Working men are singly oppressed, and react to social phenomena accordingly. Working women are doubly oppressed, and hence react to these phenomena more keenly, more sharply. Looking at life through their eyes, therefore, more thoroughly tears away the covers in which society is wrapped, revealing its naked form.

Under capitalism the capitalist, in order to survive, has continually to expand production. Karl Marx identified the capitalist imperative as: '...save, save, i.e. reconvert the greatest possible portion of surplus value or surplus product into capital! Accumulation for accumulation's sake, production for production's sake.'[5] Following this supreme law of capitalism, consumption is subordinated to accumulation, and is at the lowest level the capitalist can get away with, which varies according to historical and social circumstances.

The very opposite is true of socialism. Here production and accumulation are subordinated to consumption, which consequently is at the highest level society can aspire to. Whoever controls production, whether the working class or the capitalist class, determines the relationship between production and consumption, and this determines whether society is capitalist or socialist.

Working women play the predominant role in dealing with consumption, in satisfying the needs of working-class men, women and children. Under capitalism this constitutes their double burden.

If investigation of woman's position in Russia today indicates that her needs as worker, mother, household manager, organiser of family consumption, are paramount in society, with production directed to their satisfaction, we may conclude that Russia is a socialist society. If, on the other hand, the priority of production is accumulation—in order to compete with other states, competition which may take a military form—and the people's needs, especially those of women, its more vulnerable half, are residual, we must equally conclude that Russia is capitalist, even though its capitalist form—state capitalism— varies in a number of aspects from traditional Western capitalism.

We need, therefore, to summon the evidence of women's lives

in Russia today in order to decide what form of society Russia is. This is done in Part One of this book. A good deal of this section is given over to information, as little material relating to women has reached the West to date. The descriptions show the general condition of women as workers, housewives, members of society. The facts are predominantly drawn from digests of translations of the Russian press, radio and television.

Glasnost—the new 'openness' instituted under Gorbachev —is revealing much of the long-hidden truth. To rally support against the conservative bureaucracy for his programme of restructuring *(perestroika)* in order to turn round Russia's stagnating economy, Gorbachev has been obliged to allow much greater openness about the realities of Russian life. Grabbing at the opportunity, the people from below have forced wider the chink opened up from above, allowing a torrent of information, argument and complaints to be released regarding wide-ranging aspects of daily life. These cover issues crucially affecting women's lives—work, consumer goods and services, prostitution, and such like. We have an unprecedented opportunity to learn about a reality suppressed since the early 1930s and hidden under stories of glorious women tractor drivers, parachutists, Metro builders, astronauts, and joyful women workers and peasants.

When we compare the situation of working-class women in Britain and Russia, the daily difficulties they face and through which they are largely responsible for steering the family, the similarities are striking: the double burden of working and seeing to the family, the rebuffs encountered in finding a job or holding one if you have children or are pregnant, the lack of nurseries, the discriminatory pay for women (almost the same in both countries), their alienation; the growing homelessness, the beautifully appointed housing for the wealthy while workers' homes are often overcrowded and badly maintained; the dilapidated state of schools and hospitals; the rising accident rate in public transport; the rise in food poisoning; the strain on family life resulting in high divorce rates (similar in both countries); male drunkenness; prostitution; corruption in high places on a monumental scale; the dramatic exposure of widespread and dangerous pollution, the ideology of the national interest. One could continue with the similarities *ad infinitum*; the differences are minor.

Of course Britain has a higher standard of living than Russia, which is not to be wondered at after two centuries of the industrial revolution. But if Russian standards are compared with those of the Western camp in general, which includes countries like India and Brazil, the West cannot claim superiority.

Yet the situation of Russian women workers today poses the question: why? If we go back into Russian history since the advent of industrial capitalism in the latter half of the nineteenth century, we see the inspiring march of women workers participating in shaping events and, in the process, reshaping their own selves. At the dawn of capitalism in Russia women were the most backward section of workers in the most backward country in Europe. The revolutionary activity of the working class, including that of women workers, culminated in the gigantic leap of the 1917 October revolution which briefly brought into being the most advanced social system in the world, whose activities were dictated by the needs of the workers and their most vulnerable section—women workers, and mothers and children in particular. The Soviet government at the time strained, against over-whelming odds, to make women's liberation a reality in a society aiming towards socialism

This could have succeeded if revolutions in other countries, particularly Germany, had succeeded. They did not, and backward Russia, additionally devastated by war and civil war, was isolated and threatened. In the circumstances Stalin relegated all conditions of work and daily living, needed to lift the yoke of oppression from women, to the bottom of an agenda tightly organised to catch up with and overtake in one decade what the West had achieved in a century and a half. All the gains of the revolution were eliminated, including the efforts at women's liberation, in fact any discussion at all of the woman question.

Part Two of this book deals with the rise of women and the revolution which inspired such hopes of liberation, and their fall with Stalin's rolling back of all their gains. What happened between Stalin's accession to full power at the end of the 1920s and today has been the subject of much debate and varying interpretations. Stalin called his system the achievement of socialism, and implied in this the liberation of women. This book aims to prove the very opposite: how Stalin's introduction of the Five Year Plans at the end of the 1920s, with their heavy emphasis on 'accumulation for accumulation's sake, production for production's sake', in fact constituted a counter-revolution, reintroducing capitalism—in a different form indeed from pre-revolutionary times, the form of bureaucratic state capitalism. Women, as under capitalism everywhere, were again oppressed and carrying their double burden. Although there were superficial changes under the later leaders, Khrushchev and Brezhnev, the system itself did not change nor did the position of women.

The similarity for women workers between Western capitalism and Russia is thus not to be wondered at, since the motive force of both societies is revealed through the difficulties women encounter—the race after production and accumulation at the expense of people's needs.

But Russia is no longer the immutable monolith it appeared to be. *Glasnost* has opened many doors. Do the reforms aimed at by Gorbachev's restructuring—*perestroika*—have anything to offer Russian women? Our final chapter analyses the problems facing Gorbachev, his attempts to come to grips with them through *perestroika* and *glasnost*, and the contradictions his reforms enter into. It discloses his view of the 'woman question', and the prospects for women in this scheme of things.

Part One
Women in Russia today

Chapter one
Women and work

WOMEN are now 51 per cent of the working class in Russia. An average of only 3.6 years is taken away from work for raising children. Virtually all now work full-time, a 41-hour week.[1]

The sexual division of labour is similar to that in the West; 85 per cent of textile workers are women, 90 per cent of catering workers, 93 per cent of sewing workers, 98 per cent of nurses and nannies, 97 per cent of typists and secretaries, 75 per cent of teachers. Different to the West is that 75 per cent of doctors are women: this is a poorly paid profession. By contrast only 16 per cent of engineering and metal workers are women, 4 per cent of motor, electricity and transport workers.[2]

Officially there is equal pay. In fact, women's earnings average 70 per cent of men's.[3] This is similar to the percentage in Britain. As there is little part-time working to depress women's earnings, unlike in Britain, the lag is entirely due to skill differences, with women overwhelmingly at the lower end of the range.[4] This is not because of lower educational standards, as more women are highly educated than men, but to women's placement in jobs evaluated as requiring a lower skill. This goes hand in hand with sex segregation in employment: 55 per cent of women work in occupations where 70 per cent of the workforce are women.[5]

In many of the mass women's trades, the conditions of work are deplorable. Take one report from *Sotsialisticheskaya Industria* in January 1988, dealing with conditions in textiles, one of the major employers of women:

> The majority of factories were built before the revolution and underwent practically no modification since. There are no

shower rooms, endless queues for the few lavatories. The machines are so noisy that they exceed the legal maximum by dozens of times, hence the occupational disease of chronic hearing loss, whch affects 80 per cent of the women.

The noise also affects the women's nervous system, leads to memory loss and insomnia. But:

> Women do not bother to go to the factory clinics because they know the doctors are under orders to report a regular decrease in the number of industrial accidents and diseases. 'If you go to a doctor, you lose the rest of your health', they say.

The report claims that the trade unions have simply not informed the women that state benefits are available for those suffering from occupational ailments.[6]

One result is that difficult births among textile women are double the norm. Their babies weigh much less than average, and many suffer from oxygen deficiency. Yet the trade unions also failed to support the women when they asked for compulsory shift work to be reduced for working mothers. Also, industrial equipment operated by women is manufactured without regard for the characteristics of the female body, even though half of industry's workers are women, but exclusively 'for the statistically average male. Women sometimes have to stand on stools to adjust their machines, or lie on the machinery to work.'[7]

Factories like this one in Moscow are not operated by Muscovites, who refuse to work in such conditions, but by limitchiki—outside workers whose internal passports do not permit them the right to an apartment in Moscow, and who live in dormitories. More than 700,000 such limitchiki have been recruited in Moscow in the past fifteen years, to overcome the shortage of labour in unwanted jobs.[8] (This is readily comparable with the employment of blacks in low-paid dirty jobs in Britain in the days of its own labour shortage in the 1950s and 1960s).

Z P Pukhova, chairman of the Committee of Soviet Women, in her speech to the 19th All-Union Conference of the Communist Party of the Soviet Union at the end of June 1988, claimed that:

> Almost 3.5 million women are working in conditions which do not meet the labour norms and rules, such as in smoky,

dusty shops with high noise levels and unfavourable temperature ranges. Country women become prematurely aged through working from dawn till dusk, without days off or holidays, deprived of elementary social and everyday comforts, and the appropriate medical help. Such are the facts and they are distressing and alarming.[9]

Further evidence of the harsh working conditions of vast numbers of women workers was given by the previous chairman of the Committee of Soviet Women a year earlier, V V Tereshkova, in her report of the All-Union Conference of Women at the end of January 1987. Her report, using the latest data of the USSR Central Statistical Administration, showed that women do between 30 and 50 per cent of the heavy physical labour in the lumber, pulp-and-paper and glass industries, in light industry, in the food industry and in printing, and 26 per cent in construction.[10]

In agriculture 98 per cent of the manual workers in field cropping, vegetable growing, and orcharding are women. In animal husbandry, as elsewhere, modern methods are slow to be introduced. A typical example is shown by the complaints of women in Osipovka, a village in Buryat Autonomous Republic: 'We are working beyond our capacity. We have to carry 50-60kg sacks of mixed feed on our shoulders. We haul the manure from the livestock section manually.'[11]

Equality is not simply giving women the right to shovel manure! Where conditions of work are tolerable it is straightforward to demand equality between men and women, if it does not exist. If conditions are not tolerable, then protective legislation needs to be demanded for all workers, particularly the weaker and more vulnerable—women, youth and old workers —and an apparatus to monitor observance of the law, without which capitalism will simply flout the legislation in the interests of profit. In Britain in the nineteenth century protective legislation was hard fought for by the whole working class 'behind the petticoats of the women workers', and the trade unions did what they could to ensure proper monitoring.

In Russia there has always been protective legislation, but there is no mechanism to monitor and guarantee it.[12] Trade union organisation is of no help to women there, both because the trade unions' main effort is put into working with the authorities to fulfil the current Five Year Plan, and because women's issues are not considered of any importance.

A description by one of the workers of work in a mail transport depot at a railway station exemplifies the disregard for women's health:

> By law, women are not supposed to lift weights over twenty kilograms (forty-four pounds). But if the weight of the packages does not exceed this weight, it is assumed that a woman can lift this same weight over and over again, countless numbers of times... Thus, altogether a woman must lift more than two thousand kilograms (forty-four hundred pounds) in one shift and during 'holidays' four to five tons... In addition to this, the woman worker must walk great distances... During an average day, each woman must carry packages a total of two to three kilometres, and five kilometres on 'holidays'... If each package weighs about ten kilograms, the worker must move from 350 to 1,000 kilograms. One woman pushes this load, straining herself to avoid bothering her busy co-workers... This is not unlike the work in the pre-revolutionary salt or coal mines.

The women work twelve hours a day to fulfil the Plan. They are allowed only 30 minutes to eat in the day or night shifts. If the quota is not fulfilled, they work on. Among four teams in the packaging division there is only one man—the team leader.[13]

Besides doing heavy physical labour, women are extensively employed in night work, another area which, though allowed in Stalin's time, was again forbidden by law nearly two decades ago. As many as four million women work night shifts.[14] They can be doing so for 12 hours on end, just as on the day shift.[15]

Night work for women is grim. It is largely chosen by unskilled women to alternate with their husbands in order to overcome baby-minding problems. When the woman returns in the early hours, the day's work to serve children and husband begins. The woman is lucky if she can grab two or three hours of sleep in the day, and she becomes haggard and old before her time. Life is hard enough when work times are rostered. Where crises of plan fulfilment are so frequent, the manipulation of work-times causes even greater disruption in women's lives, particularly if they have children.

Multi-shift working is also carried on in industry. The hated 'black Saturdays'—so-called 'voluntary Saturday working to fulfil the Plan'—continue to be demanded.[16] Women are included in all these arrangements, no matter what their domestic situation. In fact workers in light industry, where women form a large bulk of the workforce, work more overtime than anywhere else.[17] Women are never asked if they want to work overtime; the extra hours are simply considered their duty.[18]

Nor are nurseries of help to many mothers, as only half the children of pre-school age can find a place in a year-round nursery; in 1986 1.5 million parental applications for places were rejected.[19] This compares well with Britain, which cannot boast nurseries for anywhere near half its children. The position is somewhat qualified, however, by the fact that practically all Russian women work a 41-hour week, while in Britain nearly half the women work part-time. This makes the need for nurseries in Russia more pressing. And even if the children are accepted in a nursery, anxiety is not eliminated, as, according to V V Tereshkova, 'the increase in the sickness rate among children in kindergartens and nurseries arouses our deep concern.'[20]

Women with children are entitled to preferential treatment at work. The serious decline in the birthrate in European Russia prompted entitlements for women with children to undertake lighter work, to a shorter working day, a shorter working week, flexi-time, time for breast-feeding at work, maternity leave and extra holidays. These measures, however, are observed more in the omission than the commission. Hardest hit are those 'Heroine Mothers' with many children, who, having to stay home when their children are ill, suffer the consequences at work:

> People don't like to employ a woman with children, and at the interview they always show a preference for men. If a woman gets a job, they turn against her after the first sick note. The unfortunate mother turns out, as always, to be herself to blame for the fact that her child is ill! They say, 'You had the child, you have to take the consequences!' and move her to a lower paid job. After the second or third sick note, they find ways of getting rid of her.[21]

From all over the country unjustly dismissed women flock

into Moscow as *limitchiki* to seek work.[22] Tens of thousands of women also appeal to the Committee of Soviet Women, complaining of being sacked while on maternity leave, of pregnant women not being transferred to light work, of not being hired if you are the mother of small children.[23]

As in capitalist countries everywhere, West or East, women's oppression leads to their being over-represented in unskilled jobs, and under-represented in leading positions. Though over half the labour force, they occupy only one in seven supervisory positions. For instance, 70 per cent of teachers are women, but only 25 per cent of heads.[24] Women have higher educational qualifications than men, constituting 61 per cent of those with specialised higher or secondary education.[25] But in 1970 only 10 per cent of women with higher education were in highly skilled jobs, compared with 46 per cent of men.[26]

For instance in journalism women are not accepted into faculties where competitive examinations are taken, and there are no women journalists in international affairs, or among political analysts either in newspapers or on radio or TV. Among chief specialists of enterprises and associations women are found in a ratio of one to twelve.[27]

Because of the weight of prevailing attitudes and the mockery shown to women tractor drivers and other skilled women agricultural workers—despite laws, provisions, and women's efforts—it is extremely difficult for women to gain skilled jobs in agriculture. It is therefore men who are employed as administrators, agronomists, accountants, warehouse managers or tractor and combine drivers—work that is both more highly paid, and does not damage their health.[28]

In polyclinics low-paid women physicians see as many as 30 patients a day. The heads of these clinics are usually men, with a much higher salary and smaller workload. *They* can write dissertations! says an embittered woman.[29]

Again, as in capitalist countries everywhere, women in high public office are few and far between. There are no women ministers of All-Union ministries and just a handful in ministries in the country's constituent republics. Women are today 29 per cent of Communist Party members, but only 7 per cent of secretaries of district party committees.[30]

Chapter two
Housing

A KEY ELEMENT in the quality of life of working women in Russia is housing. It is still the most serious social problem, as Abel Aganbegyan, Russia's foremost economist, attests. It is the priority concern of most working people, in most areas of the country. When Gorbachev goes walkabout in the provinces, no matter what *he* wants to talk about to the people, *they* always talk to him about housing, hoping that his return to Moscow may engender changes. The acute housing situation bears down much more heavily on women, who have to carry out all the domestic chores in the most difficult conditions. Because of its importance in people's lives and its scarcity, it is also the area of greatest corruption, with stories reaching the press that are quite hair-raising.

Stalin's effort to catch up with and overtake Western production led to a massive concentration of the economy on heavy industry and to the relegation of all consumer goods and services. Housing was one of the casualties. With the Second World War adding devastation, the legacy of inadequate and poor quality housing is causing considerable strain on Gorbachev's designs for the economy.

A few facts gathered from all over the country show the acute situation caused by the ruling powers' attitude to workers' housing. The queues for housing are enormous. There are four million young families waiting.[1] The Republic of Belorussia has a population of just over ten million; it has a housing waiting list of 600,000 families, and 60,000 of these have been on the list for more than ten years.[2]

Estonia's one and a half million population includes 43,000

families and individuals in need of improved living conditions and over 50,000 living in dilapidated homes. Tajikistan, with its four and a half million and highest population growth in the country, has an enormous queue of 850,000 people needing housing or an improvement in their housing conditions, that is, nearly one in five of the population. The town of Ufa, in the RSFSR near the Urals, had 118,000 on its waiting list at the beginning of 1988; in 1986 it built 7,300 new apartments.

One result of this universal shortage is that many young families have to live apart for many years,[3] even in better-off republics such as Estonia.[4]

The shortage can also lead to competing claims for the same housing, often by different nationalities, thus helping fuel nationalist unrest. Housing shortage and dilapidation was certainly one of the issues in the Armenian nationalist uprising in 1988 against Azerbaijan.[5] The same was true in Riga, capital of Latvia. Here an almost completed nine-storey block of flats was allocated to immigrant Russian building workers, many of whom migrated to Latvia precisely to get a flat. For the first time in living memory the flats were squatted by Latvians on behalf of their countrymen who had been on the waiting list for many years. One, a 63-year-old woman, had had her name down on the waiting list since 1949; in 1967 she married and moved into her husband's flat together with his first wife's seven children. In 1980 she divorced, but had to go on living in the flat even though he brought his third wife in. 'There was nowhere else for me to go,' she said. Another squatter family with two toddlers were enjoying the space after living in a single room for four years sharing kitchen and bathroom with two old people. They had been told to leave and may have to wait fifteen more years for rehousing. Meanwhile the immigrant workers held one strike to get the town *soviet* (council) to evict the squatters, and were threatening another.[6]

The plight of the hundreds of thousands of *limitchiki*, largely women, who gravitate to Moscow to fulfil their dream—described by **Ogonyok**, a well-known radical weekly Moscow magazine, as 'a good salary and a separate apartment'—is grim. **Ogonyok** asks:

> How long must young women live as 'single girls' in these dormitories? An outside worker will normally obtain a

permanent residence permit in five or six years, and she can put her name on the waiting list for housing after ten years' residence in Moscow. This means that 20-year-old women can expect to get housing when they are nearly 40, provided that they are good workers. Until then they are supposed to live in a dormitory!

Large numbers of Moscow dormitories become permanent places of residence. *Ogonyok* continues:

Recently... the management [of the dormitory of a fine fabric mill with 2000 workers] decreed that husbands would no longer be permitted to live in the dormitories. When asked, 'What are we supposed to do, get divorced?' the director merely replied that this was not management's concern and that women shouldn't get married until they have housing. And this response from an enterprise that supposedly looks after its workers!...

Ogonyok describes life in the dormitory:

Removed from familiar surroundings and left to their own devices in a huge, strange city, many of the newly arrived female workers are doomed to casual encounters that fail to bring them happiness. And no matter what—next morning they face the rumble of the machines and the arduous monotony of their labour. After work they return to the boredom, crowding and incessant noise of the dormitory. All this causes conflicts and mutual hostility among dormitory residents. Not long ago a young single mother died in a shared room, her baby in her arms. She was afraid to ask for help from her neighbours on the other side of the chintz curtain, who had come to hate her because of the baby's annoying cries.

Not unnaturally many of the girls suffer from nervous and other disorders:

Doctors note that the young women who get pregnant usually have complications and more often than not suffer miscarriages or are compelled to seek abortions.
Those who succeed in getting a Moscow residence permit try to find a husband. But even if they do, where will the young

family live? Usually the couples have only their beds in dormitories meant for single workers. Intentionally or not, enterprise managers keep people from starting families. From their viewpoint, marriage is followed by children, which means that the woman will leave her job for at least 18 months. And she'll also need accommodation in a family dormitory.

If women don't marry by age 30, some have babies anyway, 'for themselves'... On the other hand, there are those who view their children merely as a means of obtaining a separate apartment—but it proves to be of little help.[7]

For these women workers housing does not seem to have progressed much since the time of Stalin's factory barracks.

Another form of housing is the communal apartment. This is a large apartment of between three and 23 rooms (average five or six), with several families using a common corridor, kitchen, toilet and bathroom (if there is one.) It is described by a woman writing in **Women and Russia**, the first feminist *samizdat* (underground magazine) in Russia, in 1979:

> It is a horror and a hell... It is constant noise and chaos, racket and uproar... one family—a husband and wife and two small children—who live in a room 22 square metres... do not let the children out of the room... Sometimes when I go by and look in through the open door, I see the father slowly and monotonously beating the children, punishing them repeatedly, and they don't even cry any more; they just let out little yelps, from habit. This family has been on a waiting list for an apartment for ten years, and the prospects of their moving to a separate apartment in the next few years are not good. The most horrible thing here is the hopelessness.[8]

The plight of the homeless is even worse. *Izvestia* of 13 February 1988 carried an article saying that the number of homeless, which it calls 'our new, unexpected social problem', is rising. Homeless people get the brush-off from enterprise employment offices, and as these are often responsible for housing their employees, the only place the homeless can turn to is police stations' 'special holding-and-assignment centres'. They 'are kept there for a month, then released and left to their own devices, to go wherever they please—be it to the train station, off to hang themselves, or to steal.'[9]

The combination of housing shortage problems and internal passport problems causes tragi-comic situations for large numbers of people. Vitali Vitaliev, a Moscow investigative journalist, spent the night before his wedding agonising with his prospective wife over how to solve his residence dilemma. He had Kharkov residence registration but would lose this if he applied for a Moscow registration to live with his Moscow-registered wife. If anything then went wrong he would lose the right to return to live in his native city and could find himself without any registration at all—and in deep trouble with the police. The only solution they could come up with was to bribe the marriage clerk not to put a marriage stamp in his passport. If she hadn't agreed, the couple would have postponed the marriage to another day and another clerk. It took Vitaliev two-and-a-half years to get permanent Moscow registration.

The next problem was to get his mother to Moscow after his father died in Kharkov. First she was not allowed to move till she was retired (at the age of 55), then the only exchange that could be found was with a woman who wanted to live in Dnepropetrovsk, not Kharkov; so someone had to be found who wanted to live in Kharkov. Miraculously the effort over bureaucratic *fiat* triumphed, and Vitaliev's mother joined her son in Moscow, after a long wait.[10] For how many does this effort result in failure?

Russian centralisation avoids the appalling shanty towns produced by the anarchic 'free market' in the West that scar the Third World from Sao Paolo to Calcutta. But even when Russian workers have an apartment their troubles are not over. The quality of much of the housing is poor. Gorbachev was left in no doubt about this on his visit to Krasnoyarsk Kray in Siberia in September 1988. On his walkabout women complained that it was impossible to live in the newly built flats. One woman declared: 'Within a month you get huge cracks in the floor. And the doors won't shut, either, it's dreadful, leaking cracks everywhere, and when it rains you get water all over the flat.'[11]

The poor quality of new houses was shown up starkly in the huge earthquake that devastated Armenian towns at the end of 1988. The new houses were flattened, whereas older houses built during the Khrushchev era, when there was a brief improvement, did not collapse.

Workers' apartments in Russia are small and terribly overcrowded. Nikita Khrushchev, when Communist Party general secretary from 1956 to 1964, tried to redress the balance, and indeed the rate of house-building in the early 1960s was the highest in the world. But the backlog of neglect was so great that the shortage was far from being overcome, and actual building of housing always lagged behind the promises. Even the promises were way below Western standards: for 1970 a density of two persons per room was promised.[12] This is more than three times the actual density in the United Kingdom that same year.[13]

The Russian legal minimum of housing space per person is nine square metres, called the 'sanitary norm'; this space *includes* kitchen, toilet, corridors and such like. Nine square metres is the size of a small room—without the extra areas. Although officially the average living area per person was 10.3 square metres in 1987,[14] millions of working-class people have less than the minimum space, and are therefore permitted to put their names on the housing waiting list. Thus in Ufa 36 per cent of families have less than eight square metres per person; in Kiev, Baku and Riga 26 per cent have less than five square metres, and in Odessa 23 per cent have less than four square metres.[15] As a comparison, the average figure for Ireland *in 1949* was 17 square metres per person.[16]

One outcome of the terrible housing situation is that anyone who can climb out of the pit through having money and/or bureaucratic clout makes prodigious efforts to do so. Housing, therefore, more than any other aspect of life, engenders corruption. In all countries housing is in short supply and corruption in housing allocation is endemic. The scale of the corruption is proportional to the shortage, and in Russia it sometimes reaches gargantuan proportions.

A vignette from Gorbachev's walkabout in Krasnoyarsk Kray neatly encapsulates the situation. A woman in the crowd complained about the lack of kindergartens. Gorbachev proclaimed: 'Such funds are being allocated here! So much has been done.' To which the woman replied: 'Then the Chairman of the Town Executive Committee should be asked about how those funds have been used and on what! And how can I approach him and ask him? His roof is not leaking, he lives in nice conditions, he is driving around in a car.'[17]

For the great majority of people housing is allocated either by the local *soviet* or the enterprise that employs them. A Communist Party Central Committee review of 'violations of social justice in housing distribution in a number of republics, territories and provinces' revealed some of the everyday miscarriages rife in the housing allocation sphere:

> Certain management personnel... illegally allocate housing to outside organisations in exchange for various services, keep a considerable amount of housing space in reserve that is later turned over... to people whose housing... already conforms to the norm, and fail to fill vacant residential buildings, apartments and rooms for inadmissibly long periods.
> Some... Executive Committees and enterprise and organisation officials use part of their housing space for such... purposes as offices, departments and institutions.[18]

In Frunze, the capital of Kirghizstan, the

> City Soviet Executive Committee circumvented the existing waiting list to satisfy the requests from the business managers of Kirgizia's Communist Party Central Committee and Council of Ministers, setting aside 78 apartments for that purpose, which were then distributed to citizens who already had well-apponted housing...
> Last year Kharkov Province and City Soviet Executive Committee ignored waiting lists in assigning 60 apartments with upgraded interiors... Some party and *soviet* officials turned their former apartments over to their children's families.[19]

There is a wide network of brokers who 'provide services' in locating apartments, for which they charge exorbitant prices. The practice is totally illegal but obviously worth the risk of a prison sentence, since the operator goes straight back to work after release. In Kiev, one Usik-Naidash is prosperous enough to keep five employees on salaries in his illegal exchange bureau. On arrest he was stripped of 100,000 roubles. In Moscow various brokers were convicted, one an inspector in the city's own apartment exchange bureau.[20]

There are innumerable examples of corruption on a gigantic scale. For example in Turkmenia the magnificent housing complexes of the former first secretary of Ashkhabad Province Party Committee, the chairman of the State Prices Committee and chairman of the Turkmenian Republic State Security Committee and other ministers and officials, could each accommodate children's institutions of many hundreds. Meanwhile 'hero-mothers and mothers with babes in arms don't receive even 0.5 per cent of the new housing stock' in the capital Ashkhabad.[21] There are 23,600 people on the waiting list, constituting over a quarter of the families in the town.[22] Kindergarten space is needed in the town for at least 30,000 more children.[23]

A letter from the town of Firyuza in Turkmenia says of the expensive homes:

> ...after all, these gentlemen have lived here just three months. And they live in such a way that some of them have watchdogs that have it better than many people in Firyuza.[24]

Another major cause of insufficient and inferior housing for workers is the tie-in of housing construction with enterprise and farm funds. Many large enterprises are responsible for providing housing, kindergartens, clinics, shops and cultural activities for their employees, and are funded accordingly. With the constant pre-occupation of management with the fulfilment of the Plan, there is neither time nor inclination, nor funds left, to bother with the non-productive aspects of the enterprise. Housing, being the workers' priority need, shows up in starkest form the subordination of consumption to accumulation. Working women, who look after the home and its occupants, suffer the consequences disproportionately severely.

In Britain poor working-class families and the not-so-poor in some areas of the country are well aware of the housing shortage —of the homelessness, overcrowding and rotten maintenance of much working-class housing (in common with other advanced countries, let alone those in the Third World). The race for profits causes the same neglect of housing in all countries. But the rapidity of Russia's economic expansion in the first decades of the Five Year Plans pushed Russia's housing problem to the extreme.

No matter that couples live apart in intolerable conditions, that ethnic confrontations take place for scarce housing space, that people become demented from despair—so long as those victims fulfil the production plan and yield the profits! For the Russian bosses, workers are merely labour power needed for the accumulation of capital.

The television announcer on Gorbachev's visit to Krasnoyarsk Kray eloquently described the government's priorities and the people's reactions:

> Alongside the gigantomania in construction of mines, factories and works, the social infrastructure, the development of housing and provision of food have often appeared like pigmies. And however some people might like to avoid real sharpness in talking about simple human everyday life and affairs, however grandiose the figures and production reports might sound, this is precisely what people started talking to the general secretary about.[25]

Chapter three

Consumer goods

THE SATISFACTION of human material needs depends on the availability of goods and services, which in turn depends, in a state-controlled society, on the priority given by the state to their production. That again depends on which class controls the state. Marx wrote in **The Communist Manifesto**:

> In bourgeois society, living labour is but a means to increase accumulated labour. In communist society, accumulated labour is but a means to enrich, to widen, to promote the existence of the labourer.

It is by this criterion that capitalist countries are adjudged capitalist; by the same criterion Russia must also be adjudged capitalist.

As regards consumer goods and services the situation for workers in the Western countries and Russia shows a marked similarity—and radical differences. The similarity lies in the inability of workers to buy a vast range of necessary or desirable goods and services. The differences lie in the reasons why they cannot buy them. In the West most goods and services, while adequate in supply and usually in quality, are too expensive for most workers' wages, and choice is therefore limited. In Russia basic commodities such as food, rent, transport and energy are cheap, but their shortage is chronic and their quality often poor, so choice here too is limited. In both regions the rich are able to buy the quantity and quality of goods they want.

The legacy of Russia's relative backwardness means that workers there do not have many of the commodities available to those in the more advanced countries of the West, such as cars, though the situation levels out when countries such as India and Brazil are added to the balance.

It is well known that in Russia there are some goods and services that are more than adequate in supply and tip-top in quality, for example armaments. It is equally well known that goods and services for the mass of the population do not fall into this category. If accumulation did not produce consumer goods for the working people, it did produce the weapons to ensure that the bureaucracy would not lose to international imperialism the means of production it controlled.

The low priority given to consumer goods and services acutely affects working-class women, increasing their double burden, their yoke of oppression. Tradition, and the six decades of total neglect of women's issues, dictate that women do all the caring for the family, husband and children, and the attendant domestic chores. Despite constant campaigns on all sorts of topics to shape people's attitudes, there is no effort made to encourage men to help in the home. Rather the opposite.

'Women's work' in Russia is extremely taxing. Enormous numbers of hours are spent on it, inside the home in terribly cramped, often insanitary conditions, and outside in queues for all necessary consumer goods. In addition, public services are poor, transport is overstretched, works badly, and is prone to accidents, particularly in the big towns, and the journey to and from work therefore consumes a lot of energy. Pukhova summed up the situation at the 19th Party Conference:

> The present-day consumer service is virtually incapable of helping the family, its network is underdeveloped, there are extremely few services and they are beyond the means of many.[1]

The result is that women spend 41 hours a week at work, and 40 hours doing domestic chores (30-35 in towns, 55 in rural areas).[2]

Shopping is an irksome, time-consuming burden, involving hours of queueing. Shortages are universal. Supermarkets are rare, and shopping generally involves visits to several small stores (bakery, dairy, fruit and vegetable shop, butcher) where the women wait in three queues: one to order, one to pay, one to receive the goods. In the street they need to be on the constant lookout for black marketeers selling hard-to-find items such as toilet paper or oranges. **Women and Russia**, which describes the shopping expedition, advises: 'Patience, or the willingness to stand two hours in a line, and preparedness (all Soviet women carry a net bag to hold unexpected purchases) are the key.'[3] When unexpected items appear, women try to buy up for acquaintances too. The resulting barter activity takes up extra time.

Delegate Zakharova lamented to the 19th Party Conference: 'What question can there be of my development as an individual when I spend much of my time as a housewife standing in a queue?'[4] And she is not among the lower levels of working-class womanhood. **The Economist** reckons that a housewife in Omsk probably has to spend at least six hours longer doing her shopping each week than a housewife in Omaha in the USA.[5] 'Small wonder that women say they rest up from their household duties while at their government jobs.'[6]

The scarcity and shoddy quality of consumer goods may be illustrated by a description of fruit and vegetable provision in the capital, Moscow, which is in general better served than most other places. Both supply and quality are so poor that on 21 September 1988 a crisis meeting was held involving the very highest bureaucrats of the party and the *soviets*: Zaykov, member of the Politburo and secretary of the CPSU Central Committee, first secretary of the Moscow City Party Committee; Murakhovsky, first deputy chairman of USSR Council of Ministers and chairman of the USSR State Committee for the Agro-Industrial Complex; Sklyarov, head of the agitprop department of the CPSU Central Committee; and others at the very top of the state apparatus. All who spoke acknowledged the acuteness of the situation:

> ...at the very height of the season [September, the harvest month] the queues for fruit and vegetable produce in the capital are getting no shorter. Shop shelves are frequently empty. The quality of vegetables, fruit and potatoes is poor, and a considerable amount is simply rotting without even reaching the consumer.[7]

There are too few lorries (about half the number needed), and a serious shortage of storage facilities, so food rots in the fields, in open trucks in railway sidings, in elevators (where grain even sometimes explodes).[8] Very often local State Agro-Industrial Committee inspectors do not check produce which is being sent a long way. Refrigerated trucks 'are going back and forth across the whole country carrying fruit and vegetables and through... criminal negligence thousands of tonnes of produce grown by our state and collective farm workers are going to waste.'[9] Losses in harvesting and storage amounted to the enormous figure of *one-fifth* (for grain and fodder)[10] or up to *one-third* (for vegetables).[11]

In addition to the losses at source and in transit, a good part of the actual delivery to the city is sub-standard. In the first eight months of 1988, 63,300 tonnes of produce or 11.4 per cent of all deliveries were substandard. A number of consignments of fruit and vegetables also had an excessive nitrate content from the over-use of chemical fertilisers.[12]

It is ironic that the shortage and poor quality of produce is contributed to by a shortage of instruments on the farms to determine their quality.[13]

The supply of other basic foodstuffs is also poor. Gorbachev in his visit to Krasnoyarsk Kray in Siberia in September 1988 remarked on the inadequacy of meat supplies, which, after allocations to public catering, children's establishments and hospitals, leave very little for open trading; and that despite the fact that there is twice as much arable land *per capita* in the region as in the country as a whole there is a shortage of food.

The shortage has forced the introduction of meat rationing in nearly a third of the RSFSR, the largest of the fifteen republics with a population of 143 million.[14] Sugar is also widely rationed.

Reports of shortages in other basic foods abound. For instance, in Sakhalin, a far eastern island and centre for the Soviet Pacific fish industry, there is a shortage of fish![15]

Besides food, there are shortages of every type of everyday requirement and long queues when these unexpectedly appear. Soap and washing powder are extremely short—giving rise to the phrase 'socialism with a dirty face.'[16] Even miners, after seven hours at the coalface, cannot get a bar of soap to clean up with. One of the miners in the big Kuzbass miners' strike of July 1989 remarked: 'How can I describe how humiliating this all is?'[17]

Items which, according to *Izvestia*, never reach the shops include textiles for dresses and other clothing, children's garments, men's suits, jackets and trousers, dresses, blouses made of cotton and blended fabrice and many types of knitwear and footwear.[18] Zakharova, from a mining combine in the north, complained that in her *kray* (region), 'where it is winter for nine months of the year, you cannot even get a full set of multivitamins at the chemists, and people have to walk around in more than 50 degrees of frost wearing clothes made from synthetic fur.'[19] When Gorbachev visited Norilsk in the Arctic Circle, he was made fully aware by the people of the inadequate supplies of warm clothes, especially for children. To get fur coats, boots, footwear in general, people have to go to Central Asia (which is *not* in the Arctic Circle).[20]

There is a particularly acute shortage of articles for children and young people. This is a direct result of the Plan's irrational accounting system which orders in gross quantities of rubles and amount of cloth used rather than using a more rational item-by-item costing process. It is therefore more profitable to make fewer large articles than more small ones. A survey of 105 towns showed that in a majority (between 50 and 75 per cent) there were no children's pyjamas, jackets for children of creche age, boots, raincoats for children of school age, cotton skirts and jackets, and everyday and party shoes. And in many towns (between 30 and 46 per cent) there were no suits for children of creche age, no blouses or skirts, no jeans for children of pre-school age, or cotton suits for schoolchildren.[21]

Shortages are bad enough. When poor quality is added to poor supply, life is indeed hard for women. A check made at the USSR Ministry of Trades wholesale bases showed that 10.4 per cent of goods checked were substandard, including 4,300,000 pairs of leather shoes.[22] Altogether some 1.4 billion rubles worth of unwanted and unmarketable goods in outmoded fashions, models and designs had accumulated in the trade network.[23]

Domestic appliances present, if anything, a worse picture. **Sovetskaya rossiya** reported on 23 December 1988: 'The list of goods in short supply is growing. It is difficult to buy colour TVs and tape recorders, and it is almost impossible to buy video-tape machines. Washing machines and refrigerators have disappeared.'[24] The washing machines that do exist are small and inefficient, dryers and laundromats rare. The average Russian woman resorts to the time-honoured technique of boiling clothes on the stove to get them clean. In the countryside the sight of women washing clothes in the local pond is not uncommon.[25]

Before *glasnost*, the most exciting thing about watching Soviet television was that the set was liable to catch fire. Fires from television sets rose by 69 per cent between 1980 and 1985.[26] Enormous numbers of appliances need to be returned during the period of their guarantee—of the order of one-and-a-half milllion television sets or clocks in the first half of 1988 alone.[27]

Prices for manufactured articles are high, many well beyond the means of ordinary workers. To buy a small car takes an average five months' pay in the USA, eight months in London or Paris, nearly four years in Moscow. The queue for cars is eight years long. Then the car will break down more often, and spare parts will be much harder to find.[28]

Even according to official figures the consumer economy is not improving. The USSR State Statistics Committee reported that sales of some individual commodities in state and co-operative trade for 1987 (the latest report out) were down compared with 1986: fish by 2 per cent, margarine 1 per cent, potatoes 1 per cent, vegetables 5 per cent, clothing, underwear and fabrics 3 per cent, footwear 5 per cent, refrigerators 3 per cent, television sets 6 per cent. Sales of other products were the same as 1986 or slightly up. But the population increased in that period by just under three million people (to 284.5 million), so any production increases were thus negated and production decreases exacerbated.[29]

Servicing for apartments and appliances is almost impossible to get through state agencies. Once again revealing their neglect for workers', particularly women workers', needs, only six out of 47 ministries and departments that should provide paid services to the population fulfilled their planned assignments.[30] Small-scale private enterprise by individuals and co-operatives is intended to plug the gaps—and incidentally subvert the black market—but there is great resentment that these compete with state firms for scarce resources, buy state products—thus lengthening queues at state shops—and resell at high prices. They are supposedly not allowed to exceed state prices by more than 30 per cent, but Gorbachev himself remarked that they charge double, treble or even five times state prices.[31]

In any case, co-operative shops and services are a drop in the ocean of chronic shortages. At the end of 1987 co-operatives were supplying less than 0.04 per cent of all goods and services.[32] They deliver no benefit at all to working-class women and men.

A further drain on consumer goods from state shops is brought about by the by-passing of state shops and their queues. A letter to **Pravda** on 17 January 1988 complained about the cars of city party and council officials outside meat plants, fish farms, warehouses—'but you don't meet these elected representatives in queues!'[33] In addition theft and corruption are perpetrated on a big scale, largely by organised criminal gangs, encouraged by inadequate storage facilities. **Pravda** reports:

> ...a certain Ibragimov caused losses of R1,500,000 through shady dealings involving rotten onions [!], yet he is being admitted as a candidate member of the CPSU. We can hardly hope to establish order with cadres like that.[34]

What is not in short supply is rising expectations, fed by a number of factors. First, there is Russia's ability to produce adequate supplies of first-class products when they constitute a competitive or prestige priority: armaments, space stations, underground transport systems, exhibition buildings, cultural and sports showplaces, posh hotels.

Secondly, wages rose by 8 per cent in 1988 while production rose by only 2.5 per cent. So workers have more money and no outlet for it. Deposits in savings banks consequently increased by 24 million rubles in 1987 and much more since, constituting great pressure on demand.[35]

Thirdly, the printing industry does not hold back from producing glossy catalogues of consumer goods. 100,000 copies of a luxurious 'Bulletin of Trade and Industry' were printed, offering every possible consumer item: 'Ultra-fashionable clothing. Elegant shoes. Various items of haberdashery. Perfumes and cosmetics of every type. Domestic appliances in no way inferior to foreign models. And next to each beautiful picture is a description of the item, its price and the name of the enterprise which produces it.' The only problem is, they never reach the shops. Instead, 'the catalogue merely gives rise to anger and annoyance among the ordinary customers'[36]—as can well be imagined.

Even the figures given for the fulfilment of the Plan mislead expectations, as they are given by volume and price, and take no account of rejects, poor quality or theft. They may also include the same article more than once, as its sale and resale both count in the grand total.

Any attempt to change things is riddled with contradictions. Take the attempt to reform the quality of consumer goods. There used to be a mark of quality, a five-pointed star. This has almost vanished. In its place has come the letter N—'for novelty, an especially fashionable article'—at a much higher price. With Plans fulfilled in ruble figures, factories have an incentive to meet targets by producing a few expensive goods, rather than cheap items. N-products rose by 46 per cent during the first six months of 1988. The result: popular cheap products disappeared from the shelves. So although the total volume of output under the Ministry of Light Industry increased by 8 per cent (in retail prices) in the first half of 1988 compared with the corresponding period of 1987, the increase was entirely expensive N-marked items. This contributes greatly to the chronic shortages.[37] Together with wage rises, it also contributes to hidden inflation (variously estimated at climbing up to 9 per cent) despite the declared official stability of prices.[38]

And there is no guarantee that the N-mark ensures quality. Sometimes it is simply a price mark-up.[39] Lithuania, for purposes of price mark-ups, fakes foreign labels reading 'Made in USA', or Britain, or Japan.[40]

Or take the question of exports of domestic equipment. With bad harvests grain has had to be imported, and because of the slump in oil prices—Russia's chief means of acquiring hard currency— exports have been encouraged. Thus in the first eleven months of 1988 the entire increase in refrigerator production went for export. The result: the supply of fridges to Russian shops decreased by 18 per cent, and in 1989 only 55 per cent of demand was expected to be met.[41]

The brunt of all this is borne by Russian women.

Chapter four
Health

ONE AREA of Russian life which shows grossly the residual nature of working-class interests, compared with the pressure to capital accumulation through the fulfilling of the Plan, is public health. Again women workers carry the extra burden resulting from neglect. The neglect takes two forms—of commission and omission, the former being decisions about the adequacy of hospitals, clinics and other health provision, the latter a lack of decisions on health and safety which leads to accidents, illness and environmental pollution on a vast scale.

Hospitals used by those who do not pay for medical care are generally in a terrible state. For instance, in the Moldavian Republic *Pravda* reports that 'many polyclinics and outpatient facilities are located in ill-suited and even dangerous premises.'[1] The paper also describes a clinic in Ashkhabad, capital of the Turkmenian Republic:

> For the past three years [it] has been without hot water in the summer, so that outbreaks of infectious diseases are a high probability. The lights often go out during operations! Cold water outages are rampant. The Ashkhabad Province Agro-Industrial Committee has refused to provide direct shipments of fruits and vegetables.

In the ten years the clinic was under construction, pipes and radiators (which someone had the bright idea of putting inside the wall panels) have rusted out. The rooms are constantly wet and are plagued with mildew.[2]

This is the clinic of what is called the Turkmenian Republic Ministry of Public Health's Institute for Protecting the Health of

Mother and Child!

There is, besides, a terrible shortage of clinics and maternity homes in the town. Because of indifference on the part of the Soviet Executive Committees towards the repair work needed in hospitals, doctors often have to do the repairs themselves instead of treating patients.[3] *Pravda* reports:

> This is the situation in the capital. Imagine what it must be like in the countryside! A Krasnovodsk hospital for treating infectious diseases is located in a building that was once a stable! Over 60 per cent of maternity clinics, maternity wards and children's hospitals lack hot water, 127 hospitals have no running water, and about two-thirds of them lack sewer lines. And on top of that, the septic tanks (and, if you'll excuse the term, the open cesspools) are on a level with the ground water. Those are facts, and we have to reckon with them.[4]

Gorbachev himself, on his visit to Krasnoyarsk Kray, was berated by people about the bad state of the hospitals, and told his own story, which if it were not so distressing, would be farcical:

> Viktor Petrovich Astafyev came to see me and he told me... his daughter was about to give birth to a baby—and just listen, there was a queue for the maternity home! What do you think of that then, a queue for the maternity home! She was due to give birth![5]

This neglect of state hospitals, with maternity homes, a basic requirement for women, at the bottom of the pile, needs to be seen against the effort put into the luxurious prestige projects that were built in the same regions. Akhmadzhan Adylov, an agro-industrial director in Uzbekistan, spent millions of state funds for his sumptuous lifestyle with impunity, while in the same republic an astonishing 46 per cent of hospitals were in buildings which did not meet the Ministry requirements for sanitation and hygiene.[6]

To give 'the construction project of the age', the Baikal-Amur Railway in Siberia, its due, a railway station of marble and timber was built in one of the towns along the line. The district hospital in the same town is housed in a barracks-like building without any conveniences. 'Well, what of it, comrades,' exclaimed Y I

Chazov, USSR Minister of Health, to the 19th Party Conference, 'the delegations will not be going there anyway. They have the Baikal-Amur Railway and all Siberia to see.'[7]

Sixty thousand inhabitants of Kazakhstan have tuberculosis —a disease proclaimed eliminated. Conditions in the tuberculosis institute in the capital, Alma-Ata, have to be seen to be believed. Yet these patients watched as close by a public bath and health centre was built in marble at a cost of 15 million rubles.[8]

A heartbreaking story is told by Vitali Vitaliev, the investigative journalist, of a visit to two children's sanatoria in the Crimean resort of Yevpatoria. In the one,

> the offspring of high-ranking officials were staying. They were for the most part quite healthy and lived under excellent conditions: neat, cosy rooms for two, beautiful playing grounds, a school, swimming pool, etc...
>
> ...at the neighbouring 'ordinary' sanatorium for children suffering from tuberculosis the conditions were awful: dirt, shabby houses, plaster peeling off the walls; mice and cockroaches.
>
> ...[at the first] the daily food ration per child was four roubles 87 kopecks. The privileged children were eating salmon and caviar, the underprivileged suffering from TB—bread and potatoes.[9]

In Moscow a hospital for invalids of the Second World War took eleven years to build.[10] An official of the Russian Republic Ministry of Social Security spoke in an interview with *Pravda* of 'the total neglect of the aged in a number of areas. Examples of "service" at rest homes, he said, were not just shameful but painful to recount: it amounts to providing water—and sometimes not even that!'[11] Minister of Health Chazov comments:

> And this picture of the attitude to the innermost needs of human beings—of which health is one—was not only true of these regions. It is sometimes said that this bitter truth has only been brought to light now and that the leadership was unaware of the situation. This is not true. Scientists, doctors, and party workers informed them of the situation. They sometimes even achieved positive decisions. But then everything subsided and collapsed when faced with reactions

like this: yes, you have stated the issue correctly, but today there are other, higher state interests and you must wait. So they waited. The result is the very serious situation in public health care we have inherited today and which will take more than one five-year plan to put right.[12]

In these circumstances of neglect, it is no wonder that infant mortality is high. In Turkmenia infant mortality is called 'a communal disease'. 'Jaundice cases are up 62 per cent', there are epidemics of viral hepatitis, and intestinal infections, especially for pregnant women and babies, are rampant. The latter two account for 80 per cent of infant deaths. Yet there is not a single children's hospital for infectious diseases in the republic.[13]

Chazov accused the Uzbek Communist Party leader S Rashidov, who was involved in housing corruption, of not lifting a finger to save the 33,000 children less than a year old who die annually, out of a population in the republic of 18 million.[14]

Russia is 32nd in the world in terms of life expectancy—well behind developed Western countries.[15]

Food poisoning in a modern society, as we have seen in Britain, is the outcome of putting profits before people's health. In Russia the incidence of intestinal infection is high: 1.7 million people are seriously ill every year as a result of 'poor water supplies, the low level of sanitation and hygiene at many dairy and meat processing enterprises and the low level of sanitation generally.'[16] The number less seriously affected will be many times this.

The relationship between profits and women and children's well-being is well illustrated in an article in *Literaturnaya gazeta* on 23 March 1988 on tobacco growing and processing:

> On 13 September 1987, an ambulance brought Adolat Sobirova to the Pendzhikent Central Maternity Hospital. Although she had suffered a miscarriage five days before, she hadn't gone to a doctor—it was the height of the tobacco harvest. Her hands were stained black from tobacco juice. It wasn't the first sign of trouble—in late 1986 Adolat had given birth to a stillborn child. But the tobacco took precedence over everything!

Health was a secondary issue.

The incidence of illness among children in this region increases sharply when the tobacco-harvesting season begins, as do various ailments among women. One of the most common is anemia. It afflicts roughly 70 per cent of the women in rural areas where tobacco is grown.

Safety was a secondary issue.

The tobacco harvesters' working conditions are difficult and dangerous. They inhale nicotine, ammonia and methanol. Pesticides and tobacco juice have a harmful effect on the skin, as does the tobacco dust with its fibrinogenic, allergenic and generally toxic effects. All these things cause ailments of the skin, eyes, and respiratory, digestive, cardiovascular and blood-production systems.[17]

But not one administrative department has ever studied the effects of tobacco on the health of women and children. Why? The vice-chairman of the Leningrad Collective Farm gave the answer: 'Every year the crop yields between two million and two and a half million rubles in net profits. Tobacco is the most profitable crop.' It is more profitable than vegetables, orchards or vineyards. So—away with them! Previous walnut, apricot and apple orchards were uprooted and tobacco substituted. Happily for the farm chairmen, they are not responsible for farmworkers' health, but only for the harvest, in other words the profits.

To make these profits women and children work from five or six in the morning:

At five in the afternoon, after their midday break, they're back in the fields, and they stay there until dark. When they get home, instead of taking up books or lessons or even watching television, they bind the leaves into bundles before finally going to bed. And so it goes, day after day, until the last tobacco leaves are harvested.

None of the profit has been used to mechanise labour or protect the health of women and children. The elementary reforms suggested by the Director of the Tajik Research Institute for the Protection of Mothers and Children—an ubiquitous organisation ever-present side by side with conditions for mothers and children that are appalling—illustrate the brutality of the profit drive: it wants to ban the use of children and young girls on tobacco plantations, and organise mandatory twice-daily meals fortified with vitamins, to be paid for by the farms.[18]

A story from Turkmenia shows the same conditions in cotton-growing there, and the same concern about profits by the farm chairman. The **Pravda** correspondent writes:

> At the Moscow Collective Farm in Kaakhka District of Ashkhabad Province we saw how unsmiling women, loaded down with fertiliser sacks, shuffled heavily through the field. 'The young plants are in bad shape,' farm chairman A Aimamedov said dejectedly. 'We have to give the cotton some support.'

Who will provide support for the women—our mothers?[19]

The same interest in the quantity of the harvest to the exclusion of all else is shown in melon production in Turkmenia. The two Deputy Ministers of Health and the head of the Communist Party Central Committee's Department of Higher School Research admitted that they have not eaten local melons for a long time—'the very same excellent famous Turkmenian sugar melons'. The reason? In pursuit of good yield figures they 'push' fertilisers—nitrates and nitrites—on the fields to dangerous levels. 'But the sanitary and epidemic administration stubbornly refuses to run checks on melons.'[20] The melons are sold to unwitting customers, who suffer for the melon-growers' profits.

The pervasive attitude of not caring, neglect, cynicism, has resulted in terrible tragedies, like the infecting with the Aids virus of 27 babies in a single hospital in Ebista, a town in Southern Russia. The scandal was uncovered by the newspaper **Trud**, as just one of a series of similar incidents. The cause was the use of unsterile syringes. **Trud** remarked: 'Years of ingrained cynicism have produced only more cynicism.' The health authorities tried to check medical registers to see how the syringes were used, but they went unaccountably missing. The suggestion to give the nurses disposable syringes drew this comment:

> Where's the guarantee that tomorrow she won't be doing several injections with the same disposable syringe, or selling the rest to drug addicts, as happened in Leningrad and Odessa?[21]

Compounding the danger of infection is the chronic shortage of disposable syringes. Each year 6,000 million injections are given: the Plan for 1991 is for an output of 3,000 million syringes; current production capacity is seven million![22]

In terms of the share of the gross national product going to public health care, out of 126 countries Russia is only in the mid-seventies.[23]

Most unhelpful when it comes to the danger of Aids is the attitude to sex. It is still today closely hidden behind a Victorian pseudo-puritanism. 'Our sexual behaviour,' writes an expert in *Ogonyok* magazine, 'is a bigger national secret than a map of defence establishments'. Sex education in schools usually does not exist beyond 'botany teachers giving the lessons, and using the example of flowers to explain the whole thing.'[24]

When shortages of contraceptives are added to ignorance, the prospects for women are indeed grim. The Pill is not approved for large-scale distribution and Russia does not produce its own Pill, diaphragms are scarce, intra-uterine devices scarce and expensive —120 rubles on the black market against an official price of 50 kopeks (half a ruble)[25]—condoms are scarce, and when available 'like galoshes',[26] and, worst of all, unreliable. A Health Ministry official told *Ogonyok* that under the 1988 national plan he ordered 600 million condoms from the ministry responsible for their production; the ministry cut the order to 220 million, claiming it did not have the capacity to produce more or hard currency to buy abroad (the population of Russia is 284 million). Promotion of condoms is regarded as corruption of youth.[27]

The result is that the main contraception available for women is abortion, and this is resorted to on a monumental scale.

Socialists vehemently defend a woman's right to choose to have an abortion or not, as women cannot be free if they cannot control their own bodies. In Britain and other countries working-class women and men have fought and won against numerous attempts to further restrict existing abortion rights, inadequate as they are. But abortion should be considered a failsafe if ignorance or mishap has resulted in unwanted pregnancy, not as a standard contraceptive measure, since repeated abortions are bad for women's health and their future chances of having children.

Abortion was legalised in Russia in 1955 after Stalin's death.

In 1965 Russia had the highest incidence of abortions in Europe, with four out of five pregnancies ending in abortion. Most women have four or five abortions in their lifetime.[28] Tatyana Mamonova, editor of **Women and Russia**, knows women who have had 15 abortions. She describes the conditions in abortion clinics and maternity hospitals as brutal. Anaesthetics are commonly denied for reasons both of shortage and moralism (in other words as punishment). Abortions are carried out often without anaesthetics and to several women simultaneously, while others are waiting in a queue outside within hearing distance. In some clinics the women are tied to chairs.[29] In 1989 the question of abortion without anaesthetics was still a matter for discussion, confirmation and denial.[30]

With pressure on doctors and nurses from overwork in rotten conditions, poor pay and prudish prevailing ideas, the attitudes towards patients, particularly abortion patients, is notoriously cruel. Even the Minister of Health, Chazov, described it as 'heartless and irresponsible.' (Chazov goes on to say that this is a disease not only of the medical profession).[31] Neighbourhood doctors are overloaded; their manner is conditioned by the desire to get rid of patients, especially the old,[32] rather than ease their problems.

Of course there is a way—for both health workers and patients—to avoid the queues, the bad service and the nastiness: paid treatment. This exists in the state sector and is also the fastest growing industry in the new co-operative movement that is being heavily promoted by Gorbachev. More than 2,000 medical ventures were established in Moscow in 1988. The atmosphere is very different to the overloaded free clinics and hospitals. Patients are made welcome; elderly people are particularly pleased.

There is a higher proportion of doctors per institution in the medical co-operatives than in state medical organisations, they are better paid,[33] and doctors feel that it gives them 'the opportunity to use more fully their professional skills.'

The popularity of private health care has pushed the price up astronomically. At the beginning of 1986, in the paying state sector, it was 50 kopeks to see the physician, and three and a half rubles for a consultation with a professor. The co-operatives charge up to 60 rubles or more for a single visit—almost a third of the average monthly wage.[34]

And just as co-operatives in general do not flinch from appropriating state equipment and sometimes state time, so too do the medical co-operatives, thus further reducing the resources for health care for the mass of the population dependent on the national health service.

Top people do even better. As the sociologist Leonid Gordon said: 'We have spas and clinics where, for all the money in the world, no ordinary citizen will ever be able to send his son for treatment.'[35]

Chapter five

The family

FOR CAPITALISTS the worker's family is a cheap way of daily refreshing labour power and of reproducing and socialising future labour power for the needs of accumulation.

For the working class the family is a haven against the rigours of the outside world. But the very walls which shut out the stresses, also shut in whatever strains arise between the family members. When conditions are cramped, material needs irksome and time-consuming to satisfy, and relaxation minimal, the strains can become intolerable, the family turn into a hell and burst asunder.

The difficult conditions of everyday life for working-class people in Russia puts great strain on the family. If the prudish attitude to sex dictates marriage because of the woman's pregnancy, which is the case in about half of young people's marriages in large cities,[1] we should not be surprised at the prevalent instability of the family. Divorce rates are high. One-third of marriages nationally are dissolved,[2] and in Moscow, Leningrad and other big cities, over a half.[3] With nearly all women working full-time, and basic foodstuffs, rent, transport and other facilities when available very cheap, their greater economic independence enables them to cut unwanted ties. The big majority of divorces are initiated by women, over a half because of the man's drunkenness.[4]

The instability of the family results in a large and growing number of single parent families (eight million in 1984), particularly in the towns.[5] A tenth of all babies were born to single mothers in 1987.[6] If the smaller figure for the Moslem Republics (where the more traditional patriarchal family still holds sway) is excluded, the incidence elsewhere would be seen to be much higher.

In a society where a woman had the right and facilities freely to choose her family status and parenthood, these figures would not be noteworthy, but in the difficult circumstances in which Russian women find themselves, the figures spell untold misery. A **Moscow News** reporter tells of babies being abandoned for reasons of poverty—'nowhere to live with the child or money to support it'—or bigotry—'mother will not take them in, father said not to show up before his eyes...' There are 21 homes for abandoned children in Moscow, catering for 2,500 children from birth to three years, a situation which prompts the reporter to suggest that, just as long ago if one knocked at the window of a church or monastery it was possible to leave a child anonymously with church servants, so perhaps in present-day conditions it was worth thinking of something similar.[7]

Another consequence of the heavy strain on the family is the fall in the birthrate from the 1960s onwards. The annual birthrate fell from 25 to 17 per thousand of the population in the single decade of the 1960s.[8] Again this figure masks the huge variations between the European Slav and Baltic states and the Moslem Republics of the south and Central Asia, where the population numbers over 50 million. While in the former the norm is one or two children per family, in the four Central Asian Republics a quarter of the families have more than seven children; the population there grew by about a third between 1970 and 1979,[9] and is continuing to grow rapidly. While the natural population increase for the whole of Russia between 1984 and 1987 was 2.9 per cent, it was as high as 8.7 per cent in Uzbekistan and 10 per cent in Tajikistan. At this rate the Moslems will represent a good quarter of the population by the turn of the century.[10]

The idea that the family will wither away under communism is officially answered as follows: 'In order to build communism and a communist family, we must strengthen the traditional family for the time being. Such is the dialectic!'[11] Also according to officialdom, the previous misconception that public child-rearing was 'more healthful, effective and correct than the family system... has cost us dearly.'

The strengthening of the family presupposes the strengthening of the gender stereotypes within it. Hence, far from the press, radio and television campaigning for men to take an equal part in doing the domestic chores, the opposite is the case, and the opposite the reality. Propaganda for sex differentials starts from birth. Teachers are told: 'train and train again, girls to be girls and boys to be boys.'[12] A Russian pedagogue spells this out for boys:

> The strength of man, to which Marx gave such significance [sic!]... must be developed from earliest childhood. Strength is one of the basic traits of man... A weak body, a cowardly and timid character, and frailty of spirit are the most negative results of bad upbringing of the boy... Even the food of the boy begins, from the age of fourteen or earlier, to be distinguished by fewer sweets and porridge, and a larger portion of meat. The boy's bed is harder, the mother's caresses are more restrained, the look of the father is more stern and punishment is stricter. And especially important is the continuous increase in the physical load, especially the workload.[13]

For the girl: 'All paths are open to her, but especially those connected with women's nature—treatment of the ill, upbringing and teaching of children and so on.'[14] The differentiation goes on through school, where boys are taught metalwork and machine construction, girls sewing and typing. The emphasis for girls is on femininity, nurturing, caring, and on women's biological aptitude not only to reproduce, but also to bring up children.

Women and Russia gives a more materialistic explanation for family-worship: 'To control the personal lives of citizens, it says, the government identified a vehicle, and that vehicle was the family.' It uses the family for social control over the personal life of individuals; for manipulating individuals, applying pressure in the necessary direction by their having something very dear to them; and as an economically secure cell. 'By attracting women to the workplace and simultaneously preserving the traditional family, the system deliberately condemned women to dual exploitation, at home and at work.'[15]

When it comes to child care, while there may be no waiting list for a childcare centre in Moscow, in the Moslem areas the story is very different. In Uzbekistan, for example, by 1990 only a third of all children will have a place in a childcare centre.[16]

A little later, schools become a problem. While over the whole country, half the schools do not have central heating, running water or a sewerage system,[17] in the Moslem areas school conditions are worse. Schools are dark, cold, and bursting at the seams. Typical was a school shown on television, built in the 1940s for 180 pupils, now crammed with over 500. The plan for a new school in 1974 got as far as the foundations.[18]

The government in Moscow clearly looks with disfavour on the high birthrate among Moslems and discriminates against them in the allocation of resources for mother and child care. The family in these parts reflects the general social backwardness. The following is a description of a woman's life in Samarkand in Uzbekistan:

> In many Central Asian families, particularly in rural areas, a woman who has barely finished giving birth to her latest child is expected to get out of bed and tend to the farm animals, the garden and the kitchen stove. She must also endure sleepless nights by the cradle and the endless chore of washing clothes, usually by hand. As if that weren't enough, she must please her husband, her mother-in-law and all her other relatives by fixing them meals and catering to their whims...
>
> Moreover, if a woman has come to her new husband without a dowry, she is often persecuted by her mother-in-law, as the village looks on with silent indifference. At worst, her neighbours will condemn the 'cheap' bride and hound her with gossip.

These attitudes are instilled in girls and boys from childhood.

> Ask any female graduate of a rural school whether she was ever taught how to maintain her independence in a marriage and how to use her rights under Soviet law if the need should arise. For that matter, boys aren't taught the qualities required of a future family man—solicitude and attentiveness. On the contrary, they are led to believe that the first imperious, feudal attitudes they display are signs of male prowess.[19]

One brave 19-year-old Uzbek girl wrote to the youth paper *Komsomolskaya pravda* begging for support. She was married at eighteen, and,

> ...according to the local customs, after the newlyweds' first
> night, the groom's parents are supposed to show the bride's
> parents and neighbours a piece of white cloth. Woe to the
> bride if the fabric is unstained.
> I must emphasise that, before I met Abdurakhmon, I avoided
> young men. Then came that fateful night! My husband
> changed radically and began to insult me and threaten that
> he would tell the whole town that I was not an honest
> woman... In the morning, Abdurakhmon told his mother
> everything. That same evening, his parents invited mine to
> come to their house... I was ushered out of the groom's house
> and returned to my parents...
> I had to prove my innocence twice: the first time to my
> parents, the second time to law-enforcement agencies. The
> doctors found in my favour. How many young women in our
> area have suffered (and are still suffering!) grief, mental
> anguish and disgrace as a result of this ill-fated scrap of
> material? Some, unable to stand it, douse their bodies with
> gasoline or solar oil and immolate themselves, others hang
> themselves, and still others take poison... It's hard for me to
> go on living.

The *Komsomolskaya pravda* correspondent informs us:

> What about the Davronov family? Everything's fine! They are
> heroes. The father, a member of the CPSU since 1952 who
> worked for many years as chairman of the Vabkent District
> Soviet Executive Committee, shrugs his shoulders: ... Ask
> anybody; they will all say we're right.[20]

It doesn't seem as if much has changed since the time of
Tsarism for these women—with one big difference: side by side
with this backwardness and superstition another life exists. A side
effect of the large-scale Russian colonisation of the cities in all
national areas—in the Kirgiz capital, Frunze, for instance, 54 per
cent of the population is Russian, only 12 per cent Kirgiz—is the
revolution of rising expectations, especially for young women.
This clash of the traditional patriarchal family, steeped in
religion and obscurantism, with twentieth century European ways
and institutions—mixed schools, clubs, cinemas, television in the

home—does not always resolve itself in the woman freeing herself to pursue her education and other desires. It sometimes leads to profound tragedy—the growing practice of self-immolation, setting one's kerosene-soaked body alight—which is carried out by little girls, adolescents or young women. They are called 'Living Torches'.

In Tajikistan alone such cases rose from 30 a year to 40 between 1983 and 1986. The reasons women take such desperate action are diverse, but all are connected with the religious obscurantism of the traditional family. The young girls' fathers do not allow them to go to school or study; they work in the cotton fields instead, earning money. Forced arranged marriages take their toll. Others are victims of husbands who beat them and the people who then ridicule *them* (not the beaters). Then there are 'those who could not endure the cruel struggle against superstition'; one such was a member of the Central Committee of Tajikistan's Komsomol, whose parents' suspicion, humiliating behaviour and beatings drove her to become a 'living torch'.

The head of the burn centre at City Hospital No 1 in Samarkand comments:

>...none of the local officials are interested in women's concerns or worries until a 'torch' bursts into flame... The authorities will say that the unhappy women never filed any complaints. Which is true: The majority of them silently and submissively bear their burden to the very end.
>How can we, their fathers and brothers, stand by in silence? We sell our women for bride-money and then watch them as, one after the other, they die in a burst of flames fueled by kerosene. What kind of human beings are we?![21]

The buying and selling in marriage of women has hit stormy waters—and not at all because of ideological opposition to the practice. On the contrary. It is because the price of a bride has become so high that families can in no way manage it. In Turkmenia it is now 20,000 to 30,000 rubles, or between ten and twenty years' *total* average wage. As a solution related families marry their children modestly within the family, an unhealthy practice which doubles the incidence of inherited diseases, and contributes to child mortality in Turkmenia in the second year of life being three times the national average.[22]

One of the biggest influences on family life is the drunkenness of the husband. **Women and Russia** comments: 'A lonely, despairing woman turns to the Church, while a man who has failed prefers alcohol.'[23] This mirrors the situation before the 1917 revolution. Alcohol sales account for an uncommonly large share of retail trade turnover: 16 per cent in 1984 compared to 5 per cent in Britain.

We have seen the toll drunkenness takes of marriages. Gorbachev initiated an anti-alcohol campaign in 1985. Officially the production of wine, vodka and beer has dropped by 44 per cent since 1984.[24] That is, above the counter. The result has been that the liquor shop queues—the only queues which have a predominance of men—get longer and longer, and when the doors open there is a scramble to get in. In Moscow, Volgograd, Perm, Kursk and many other cities queues number 300-500 people. In 1987 a quarter of a million people were arrested outside wine stores and sent to medical detoxification centres.[25] Before Christmas 1987 a woman was crushed to death in Petrozavadsk where two-thirds of the liquor stores had been closed down; as many as a thousand people fought to get to the front of the liquor queue.[26]

The above-counter reduction has produced a surge of under-the-counter home brewing, which is subject to a fine of 100-300 rubles. Three years after the campaign started 31,000 'alcohol dens' were discovered—no doubt many times more were not. The numbers arrested rose from 80,000 in 1985 at the start of the campaign to 397,000 in 1987.[27] It is mostly women who do the brewing, increasing the family income by its sale, but mostly men who do the drinking.

Another outcome of the anti-alcohol campaign is an increase in chemical substitutes. In 1987 11,000 people died of poisoning from this source.[28]

While known cases of alcoholism dropped by 17 per cent since 1985,[29] there were still 4,600,000 people suffering from chronic alcoholism and alcoholic psychosis who were registered with treatment-and-prevention centres at the beginning of 1988.[30] At the same time drug addiction has increased by two and a half times since 1985.[31]

The age of alcoholics is getting lower. Drink and drugs are spreading among 14-15 year olds. Nearly one million children are sent every year to 'internal affairs agencies' for crimes or because of neglect. In Krasnodar in the south, 70 per cent of those children, when questioned, said that home brewing had forced them out since there was no place left for them in the home.[32]

Women's solace is religion, just as it was before the revolution; 75 per cent of church members are women.[33] A section of the fledgling feminist movement in Russia is steeped in mysticism and religion. One feminist, Galina Grigoryeva, describes her devotion. First she sums up life in a communal apartment in which she lived: 'In general, the communal problems in our country are the grimmest nightmares. It's a constant stress, and you could never get along without taking *valeryanka* [a tranquilliser similar to valium] regularly.'

> Her interviewer then asks: 'What's the way out of this situation? More concretely, what do you personally do to compensate for this?'
> She replies: 'Only mysticism... I couldn't manage without it... Where is the source of morality? It isn't in society. For us... the only way to draw spiritual strength is through religion.'[34]

Religion thrives in the Ukraine: 20 per cent of its 45 million population are members of the Ukrainian Catholic Church. On the second anniversary of the Chernobyl disaster, an 'apparition of the Virgin Mary was sighted'; this attracted half a million of the Catholic faithful in Western Ukraine.[35]

The yearning of the toiling masses—and particularly its female section—for a better life, latches on to any movement that offers hope of improvement, in this life or the next—and the movements can all get mixed up in one jumbled amalgam. For example, on 21 June 1988 between 30,000 and 50,000 people participated in a demonstration for the Ukrainian language, the Catholic Church and the election of delegates to the 19th Party Conference!

The needs of *perestroika* have swung the government —whose official attitude is atheism—closer to the church. The Russian Orthodox Church was given legal status in September 1988. There is no *rapprochement*, however, between the state and Islam (though this could change if foreign or internal events persuaded the state to seek a prop among the mullahs). Nonetheless when the 'surgery' of the deputy chairman of the local

Soviet Executive Committee is open on Mondays and Fridays from six o'clock till seven, on the first Saturday of the month from ten till one, and on the second Sunday of the month from nine till midday—while the doors of the mosque are always open wide to all—and the state constantly tramples on poor and harassed people's sensibilities, it is no wonder that they cling to religion, 'the sigh of the oppressed creature, the heart of a heartless world... the opium of the people,' to use the words of Karl Marx—and with it to traditionalism, obscurantism and superstition.

It is this pervading backward outlook that causes women to be so harshly oppressed in these parts that some in despair become 'living torches'. 'Atheistic work is also a fight for women', one woman party member said.[36] True, but not when it is a charade imposed from above, without a thought for the real conditions of the people who are looking for solace.

Chapter six
Prostitution

THE PREVALENCE of prostitution is a reflection not only of society's economic state but also of its motivation—whether that is the needs of the mass of the people, or the demands of the few who profit out of the trade in commodities, including human flesh. Russian history proves the truth of this statement infallibly. The oldest profession in the world has a long, ignoble past in the country, broken only once, briefly, by the Russian revolution. Prostitution disappeared between the October revolution of 1917 and the establishment of the New Economic Policy (NEP) in March 1921. As soon as an element of private property and the market were reintroduced with the NEP, prostitution once more flourished and has done so ever since. Like many another reality, the pretence prevailed that it did not exist, until *glasnost* uncovered the unpalatable truth.

Reports have reached the press from all over the country: from Georgia, Kirgizstan, Ukraine, Belorussia, from the holiday beach resorts, the ports, the railway stations, and especially the big cities: Leningrad, Riga, Odessa, Minsk, Kiev, Tbilisi, and in pride of place the capital, Moscow.

In Moscow the police hold a catalogue of 3,500 prostitutes' names. The range in ages is wide—from 14 to 70, which encompasses 'dynasties' in which a grandmother, daughter and granddaughter 'work' together.[1] A teacher in Belorussia spoke of numbers of teenagers, some as young as 13, in the business.[2] There are a number of reports of girls' involvement in prostitution before they are out of school.[3] A reporter from *Literaturnaya gazeta* on 16 September 1987 describes the scene in Petropavlovsk-Kamchatsky and Moscow:

If you walk around the streets of Petropavlovsk in the evening, you'll see them standing outside movie theatres and cafés, changed almost beyond recognition by the heavy make-up they've put on after school.[4]

The girls get picked up by kerb-crawlers.[5]

In Belorussia the highest authorities of the republic—the Ministry of Interior Affairs, the Prosecutor's Office, the Minister of Higher and Specialised Education, the Central Committee of the Belorussian Party—instituted raids after the Young Communist League reported women 'on the prowl' (including women with husbands and children) in dormitories of the Belorussian State University, the Polytechnical Institute and other educational institutes. The goings-on had been kept quiet by the institutes and by officials.[6] The Komsomol correspondent in Minsk, the Belorussian capital, remarks:

> Minsk is a relatively lucky city... The situation in Moscow, Leningrad, Riga and other major cities is much more alarming... For many years we pretended not to notice... But these women are growing positively impudent.[7]

There is an extended hierarchy in the profession, as there is in society at large. 'Beach girls' in posh foreign outfits buy vacation passes in Moscow, Leningrad, Kiev or other cities and go to 'work' in expensive resorts where Russians with plenty of money, and foreigners, frequent hotels where it costs an average of 25 rubles per day (without food) to be put up, that is, half the average weekly wage. The *Komsomolskaya pravda* correspondent remarks: 'Yes, we do have a few honest people who earn a lot of money,' such as miners from the north and timber rafters. 'They too are represented at the [posh hotel], but they feel diffident in comparison with the habitués.'[8]

The most lucrative sphere of activity for prostitutes or pimps is foreigners; 'foreign specialists' can acquire smart foreign clothes, footwear and other consumer goods unavailable to any but the richest, and also foreign currency, which is profitably exchanged on the black market, narcotics and smuggled goods. For this purpose many prostitutes specialise in foreign sailors,[9] others in industrial towns employing foreign workers, such as Zhlobin in Belorussia[10] or Volzhsky in Volgograd Province of

RSFSR, others in holiday resorts or in posh hotels in the cities. 'Spheres of influence' are often marked out with fists.[11] One paper claims a whole 'mafia' lives on the earnings of 'foreign currency prostitutes'.[12] These high-class prostitutes can afford to pay staff of hotels and restaurants for access to places where they can:

> find clients who have foreign currency; ...physicians (who supply fake documents and clandestine treatment for venereal diseases) and the tenants of apartments that the prostitutes rent for the 'work'. The same applies to the fictitious husbands, the pimps and the taxi drivers... who not only transport the prostitutes but sometimes even find them clients. In the same category are those who help the high paid 'good-time girls' buy—bypassing the official waiting lists and often illegally—their own cooperative apartments, cars in short supply, airplane tickets at the height of the summer season, and accommodations at prestigious health resorts.[13]

These women can also afford to restrict their clientele, so that their workload is reduced.

The rates of pay vary enormously according to the place in the hierarchy. At the top it can be 100-150 rubles for the evening. One 'Madam' in Moscow, Nina Mikhailova, rented several apartments in the centre of town where she charged 150 rubles per month for rent, and also took half the girls' earnings. On a good night she made 400-500 rubles. She also had a business relationship with a food store director. 'He got the use of an apartment and the "chickie" (as he called the girls) of his choice, while she received unlimited quantities of hard-to-get food items.'[14] Two Moscow prostitutes arrested in 1987 had half a million rubles in bonds alone confiscated.[15]

The hierarchy descends sharply as the women's market value in looks or age declines. About half receive 20-50 rubles per client—but these are the young attractive women who generally have only one partner a day. Streetwalkers get no more than ten rubles on the average for each service. Between 15 and 20 per cent of women get 5-10 rubles, possibly only occasionally.[16] They frequent busy places like railway stations. The 'bald spot', as Moscow's Komsomolskaya Square is called, is the last stage of the prostitute's fall. There she may get as little as three rubles. And the lowest price? A bottle of cheap wine or a glass of rotgut.[17]

The end for many prostitutes is horrific. Some get paralysed in a drunken stupor, freeze in a snowdrift and have to have their hands and feet amputated. The three-ruble prostitutes try to supplement their income by getting the man drunk, robbing him, then throwing him out of the taxi. It is no wonder that in that harsh situation stories of prostitutes murdered by their clients are not uncommon.[18]

Who are the prostitutes? A sociological study of the majority of prostitutes in Georgia in the mid-1980s showed that 70 per cent were under 30; 52 per cent were divorced; approximately half had children—so single mothers constitute a large proportion of their number.[19] In Kiev single mothers are in the majority.[20] Three-quarters had at least a secondary education.[21]

The study says 92 per cent of prostitutes have or have had jobs. However, the majority had menial or low-paying jobs. Prostitution was not their main source of income but a means of supplementing it; making ends meet was a constant concern, and four out of five said that all of their earnings went for daily living expenses: clothes, cosmetics and food being the top priorities, then their children and housing. For the schoolgirls boredom came high on the list of causes for prostitution: 'There's nowhere to go. There's nothing to do.'

The study tries to analyse the causes of prostitution, and the words have a ring of truth anywhere:

Prostitution is a result of the differences between women's aspirations for self-affirmation and self-fulfilment and the reality of their lives. What does a young woman in the big city encounter? A modest salary and also right under her nose, 'the good life'. Imported boots cost 120 rubles...

On our movie and television screens, they watch elegant heroines pursue brilliant careers—and even if these ideal women have problems on the domestic front, their apartments, cars and wardrobes leave no doubt that their lives are a success. The newspapers and magazines print stories about women workers—next to photos of the latest stunning fashions, which in real life are worn not by the top production workers but by those who know how to 'get things.' The public never looks kindly on those who aren't successful, and at a time when the consumerist mentality is so widespread, it is particularly intolerant of those who can't keep up...

Dissatisfaction with one's 'official' earnings and status is in itself no reason to engage in prostitution. The explanation lies in the distortion of consumer demand and in the fact that standards of high consumption are not linked in the public consciousness with the size of one's labour contribution.[22]

This was borne out in the results of a poll of 15-17 year-old pupils, mostly girls, in ten Moscow general-education and vocational-technical schools, conducted in early 1987. The respondents were asked which professions and types of activity provide a high income. In the list of the top twenty, prostitution tied for ninth place with jobs of director and sales clerk. It was ranked ahead of such traditionally 'lucrative' professions as diplomat, teacher, taxi driver, auto mechanic and butcher.

Hand in hand with prostitution go drug addition, drunkenness, blackmail, illegal foreign currency transactions and other indictable offences. There has been a rapid increase in drug taking among youth. For instance in Latvia in 1986, 2.2 per cent of those indicted for drugs were under 18; one year later this had risen to 32.6 per cent, and other regions showed a similar phenomenon.[23]

Blackmail is common. In one case a tenth grade schoolgirl found out that the man she had been with owned a Toyota—and this mark of wealth decided her to blackmail him for 1000 rubles for seducing a minor. Her school friend cooked up a scheme to blackmail a married man with two children for 4000 rubles.[24]

With the rise in prostitution and its accompaniments has come a rise in illness. Over the past four years VD among young people in Georgia has quadrupled, syphilis is three times the average figure for the country as a whole, with a disproportionate increase among the young. In 1986 in Tbilisi there were 78 cases of gonorrhea and 20 of syphilis among school pupils.[25] The Komsomol identified 100 girls ranging in age from 13 to 29 who frequented certain barrack areas; many had venereal diseases. In Novorossiisk a laboratory worker, herself a prostitute, tested the other girls and found two out of every four or five to be diseased.[26]

The authorities find it difficult to contain prostitution—as is the case everywhere—even if they wanted to. Hence they adopt a lax attitude and the penalties are mild: largely warnings, court appearances for 'parasitism', 'vagrancy', or the violation of internal passport rules, and insubstantial fines, then the withdrawal of residence permits, a step which can easily be baulked. As far as the authorities are concerned, prostitution was overlooked as existing 'at a time when it was common to gloss over reality and pretend that negative social phenomena no longer existed in our country.'[27] That attitude continues, with little effort made to suppress it other than in words.

The only time the authorities took decisive action was at the 1980 Moscow Olympics, when, in a moral clean-up of the capital, they drove 70 prostitutes out beyond the 101km line (many came back).

There is no doubt that the law and order brigade, including the respectable Young Communist League (YCL), take a dim view of the law and want it strengthened, with prison sentences included. They disapprove of the fact that there are no detectives on the trail of the prostitutes and their hangers-on, and that 'instead of a solitary confinement cell during investigation, these people get a fashionable hotel room, a bar and a bowling alley'.[28] There are also calls for the resurrection of YCL patrols that once combatted prostitution on the streets.[29]

There are some who take moral clean-up into their own hands. In Volzhsky, where a number of Italians work, the young 'fighters for morality' watch for and identify the foreigner, take the fallen girl away—and shear her hair. They are called 'shearers', and there is an ambivalent attitude to their handiwork—is it hooliganism, or a good job done?[30] A number of well-respected citizens indicated to the correspondent of the Komsomol paper, 'We're in favour of the "shearers". Since ancient times, fallen women have been stigmatised in Russia and their gates tarred.'[31]

Characteristic of an oppressive class society is rape, where oppressed men take their frustrations out on doubly oppressed women. Rapes are on the increase. In Belorussia, for example, they increased by over 50 per cent in 1987 compared with 1986. Nearly half the rapists are teenagers and over 70 per cent of the victims minors—including large numbers of school students. Gang rapes were reported at technical schools in Orsha, Vitebsk, Gomel and Marino-Gorst.[32]

A final indication of official attitudes to women is that the beauty contest, that insult to working women, has reached Moscow.

'Ideally a woman is expected to have children, be an outstanding worker, take responsibility for the home, and despite everything, be beautiful,'[33] writes the editor of **Women and Russia**. To show that Russian women are up to fulfilling these requirements, they can now enter a beauty contest. 'Miss Moscow 1988' took place over two months, is expected to be an annual event and to spread to other towns. Prizes were free travel passes for trips abroad, cash and gifts; 'there was even talk of an automobile.' The contestants may take up advertising commitments for foreign firms (there is no private advertising in Russia) which will bring in foreign currency.[34]

Chapter seven
By what road?

RUSSIAN SOCIETY, with women's oppression as severe as it is anywhere, cannot be called socialist. But how did this system come about? After all, a clarion call of the socialist revolution of 1917 was women's liberation, and the revolution indeed did its utmost to liberate women, even while fighting for its life against sixteen invading armies and in the most dire circumstances of economic collapse and widespread famine.

To answer the question we must look at the intensely dramatic history of working-class women since the dawn of capitalism in Russia toward the end of the nineteenth century when it was the most backward country in Europe, through their growth and participation in the revolution that overthrew the Tsarist regime and briefly replaced it with the most advanced social system in the world, and to their subordination once more when this society underwent counter-revolution led by Stalin and the new bureaucratic state capitalist class.

Part two
From Tsarism to Perestroika

Chapter one
Women under Tsarism

MARX ONCE SAID that workers can never change society unless they change themselves, and they will change themselves by struggling to change circumstances. So it was with the working women of Tsarist Russia. They were intoxicated with enthusiasm to change their abject lot, and in doing so transformed themselves. Alexandra Kollontai, a leading participant in the Russian women's movement, wrote:

> The movement of women workers is an indivisible part of the general workers' movement. In all the risings she took an equal part, alongside the working man... At a time of unrest and strike actions, the proletarian woman, downtrodden, timid and without rights, suddenly grows and learns to stand tall and straight.[1]

In the momentous events which toppled autocratic Tsarism and brought the working class to power under Bolshevik leadership in October 1917, two phenomena stand out: one, the highly advanced technology of industry resulting from the late arrival of capitalism in Russia; the other the 'greenness' of the bulk of the working class, yesterday's peasants, who came to work in the new factories. Russian industry under Tsarism was thus an extreme expression of combined and uneven development.

St Petersburg (from 1914 called Petrograd, from 1924 Leningrad—and the heart of the revolution) was unique in the world for the size of its factories. By 1917 70 per cent of the factories had more than 1000 workers, nearly half more than 2000. The 25 largest textile works (employing 78 per cent of textile workers) averaged nearly 1,400 workers,[2] while of 18,000 women in the 'chemicals' industry more than 10,000 were employed in a single plant, the giant Triangle Rubber Works.[3] The Putilov engineering works, with its 40,000 workers, was the largest factory in the world.

This concentration gave the workers enormous strength when they rose up.

There were two sorts of workers in the cities: a smallish minority of established urban workers, and a big majority of 'peasant' workers newly arrived from the countryside.

An example of the first were the skilled metal workers: all men, literate, hard to replace, respected by management and other workers, as the awed reverence of this description testifies: 'They... swore only indoors under great pressure or on payday when they got drunk—some not even then.'[4]

An example of the second sort were the unskilled textile workers: mostly women, largely illiterate, derided by management and most male workers, the lowest rung of the social hierarchy, of whom one skilled worker could remark:

> The oddness of textile workers hit me in the eyes. Many of them still wore peasant clothes ... Women predominated among them, and one never lost an opportunity to pour scorn on them. Alongside the textile workers, the metal workers appeared to be a race apart.[5]

These different attitudes to skilled and unskilled workers were deeply ingrained and stamped their mark on subsequent events.

The influx of workers from the countryside had been rapid, the number of factory workers in St Petersburg, for example, rising from 73,200 in 1890 to 242,600 in 1914.[6] More than 60 per cent of new workers were women. The war brought an even quicker increase, raising the city's industrial workforce to about 400,000 in 1917.[7] (There were 3.4 million industrial workers in the whole of Russia). One-third of the workforce at this time were women (nearly 130,000), but 83,000 of these, the greenest arrivals, were servants.[8]

Petersburg's two main industries were metalwork and textiles. Metalwork in 1917 absorbed two-thirds of the workforce, of which one-fifth were women employed in the mass production of cartridges, shells and other armaments. Textiles absorbed a further quarter of the workforce, of which the big majority were unskilled women.[9] Indeed only 6 per cent of textile workers were skilled—mechanics, supervisors, factory police, management —and these were all men.

The youth and greenness of the bulk of the workers enabled the employers to exploit them harshly. While the conditions of all the newly arrived workers were grim, those of women workers, bowed down under the weight of an oppressive tradition, of which the capitalists took full advantage, were considerably worse. Such conditions are those of any developing capitalism, whether the London of the 1830s or the slums of Peru or Indonesia today.

Workers' housing was appalling. Those in rural and small town factories lived in crowded, filthy barracks consisting of large rooms crammed with beds, often bunks. There was no bedding, and men, women and children all slept together on hay in their clothing, often in shifts. There was no ventilation, no toilets—or at best a hole in the cement—no running water.

Worse than the barracks were small structures knocked together by workers themselves, like dog kennels or chicken pens. Worst of all was the situation prevalent particularly among textile workers, where the women worked, ate and slept by their machines.

Workers' housing in the cities consisted of fetid slums huddled round the factories, covered in black smoke from the forest of chimneys, and permanently noisy from the rumble of machinery. Most were without water or a sewerage system. There were an average of fifteen to an apartment, many sharing beds in shifts. The most common accommodation was a small dark corner of perhaps a kitchen. In 1904, two-thirds of single and two-fifths of married workers lived in such corners, with over half of the families sharing a single room. Single women often had to share a corner with a single man.[10]

For these 'homes', rents were amongst the highest in Europe—and would treble during the war after 1914.[11]

In 1910 a family needed between 600 and 700 rubles a year for bare necessities. The highest-paid skilled metal workers got just over 500 rubles a year. Women got far less. The average women's wage in 1914 was half the men's; in metalwork it was as low as 44.1 per cent.[12] The gap widened towards 1917.[13]

It was common for girls to prostitute themselves to get a job in a shop, and then to continue the practice intermittently to make ends meet.[14]

The factories had little or no ventilation, hence the air was foul, they were filthy and so hot that women textile workers normally worked in their underwear, a much disliked necessity given the prevalent sexual harassment.[15] The main grievance of women workers was the daily body search carried out by male supervisors. It was not unknown for a supervisor to make a false accusation of theft against an attractive woman worker in order the more thoroughly to grope her, while often other male administrative personnel gathered round, tossing out obscenities.

Hours worked were long. Women worked an average of 11-12 hours a day in 1913,[16] but garment workers normally worked a 13-14 hour day, then often had to take work home to finish,[17] and shop assistants did 16-18 hours.[18] It was not to be wondered at that the accident rate was extremely high—in 1913 14,300 accidents were reported in St Petersburg—the highest being in metals and textiles.[19]

Absence for childbirth was usually considered a 'major truancy' for which the woman was fined. Some legal provision had been made in 1894 to have a midwife in factories with more than 100 women and a place to give birth, but the unemployment situation provided an excuse for factories to flout the law or to refuse to hire pregnant women.

As late as 1912, 75 per cent of women worked till the onset of labour; 95 per cent gave birth without any medical assistance whatsoever,[20] and they returned to work straight after. It is no wonder that 30,000 women a year died in childbirth, and that infant mortality in Russia was the worst in Europe.

Much worse off than women factory workers were servants, who came straight from the countryside into what was called 'white slavery'. They were totally degraded, allowed no private life—not even visits from husbands—had no holidays, slept in a corner of the kitchen or corridor, were fed on left-overs, and were prey to the customary sexual attacks of the men of the household.[21]

As a consequence of their harsh lives a working woman by the age of 50 looked ancient and was ill and disabled: 'She sees and hears poorly, her head trembles, her shoulders are sharply hunched over,' said a doctors' report of 1913.[22]

Russian society was extremely patriarchal. All land and other property, except kitchen utensils, clothes and occasionally a sheep or cow, belonged to the man and devolved to the sons. The patriarch ruled with an iron hand. A woman's status in a status-ridden society was lower than that of *any* adult male.

Tsarist laws explicitly permitted a man to beat his wife, and this was so enshrined in custom and practice that a Russian writer could comment that 'the absence of beating is considered abnormal'.[23] The custom was substantiated by a whip being hung on the wall above every conjugal bed.

That was the situation in the villages and small towns but it persisted when the peasant women started migrating to the cities. In 1910 a union publication commented: 'Not only the bosses view women as the lowest kind of being, male workers do as well.'[24]

The condition of Russian women workers under Tsarism was very similar to that of black women workers in South Africa today: the long hours, little time for sleeping, bribery and prostitution to get a job, low pay; the double shift from the tradition that women do all the domestic chores alone, while the husband drinks; the beatings, violence and foul language.

But things were changing. Literacy in Russia was the lowest in Europe—but rising. In 1897 only 13.1 per cent of women could read. By 1914 this had risen to over a third—and was higher still among women factory workers.[25]

Strikes were criminal offences for which workers were sacked, exiled, imprisoned, or sentenced to hard labour. Despite the oppression there was a big strike wave in the mid-1890s in which women were centrally involved. In a famous strike in November 1895 at the Laferm cigarette factory, where 87 per cent of the workers were women, 1300 women struck because new technology threatened to lower 40 women's wages and get half the workers sacked. They broke the windows and threw the machines into the street. It took 100 armed police and two fire brigades to quell this protest.[26]

The biggest strike, and the first to go beyond the bounds of a single factory, occurred in May 1896 under the banner of Social Democracy. Textile workers struck over wages and hours, the strike spreading to a fifth of the biggest factories in Russia, employing 30,000 workers. After three weeks they returned, all factories together. For the first time Social Democracy had drawn the masses into action and became a significant movement.[27]

The 1905 revolution started on 9 January when thousands of poor workers marched to plead with the Tsar, their 'Little Father', to improve their lot. Their abject servility was instantaneously transformed into outraged hostility when hundreds were gunned down by the Tsar's soldiers on what came to be known as Bloody Sunday. Mass strikes broke out in 122 cities. In October a new strike wave led to the establishment of the first *soviet*—or workers' council—in Petersburg.

The new confidence inspired women to make demands specifically for women's protection which they had been too timid to make before, and especially for mothers: paid leave before and after childbirth, creches and time off for nursing mothers.[28] The working class marched forward together: men's demands also absorbed the new aspirations, and routinely included the reduction of women's maternal burdens.[29]

The level of consciousness reached by some in 1905 is illustrated by a letter from a woman worker concerning the foul language and behaviour of many male workers: 'This is how people who are themselves oppressed by capital speak to us.'[30] This letter neatly encapsulates the unity in oppression of men and women workers, and also women workers' additional burden of oppression.

The 1905 revolution made many concrete gains for women workers, such as the ending of beatings and the daily searches. Freedom of the press was won (and widely used by women workers), a parliament (the Duma) set up, and unions, all of which automatically included women, were made legal. Brutal repression from 1907 to 1912 eliminated the concrete gains, but could not wipe out the effect on workers, including working women, of having flexed their muscles and felt their strength.

Bolsheviks, both men and women (if less prominently), had played an important part in leading the strikes. When the workers' movement recovered in 1912, they paid special attention to women workers, who in 1913-14 were leading some huge and spectacular strikes. These were not only over economic and women's issues, but also for political ends, for example against the arrest of political activists. In one celebrated case, women struck in protest against the arrest of Mendel Bailiss, a Jew accused of the ritual killing of a Christian boy[31]—a remarkable action in church-ridden, anti-Semitic Tsarist Russia.

For International Women's Day in 1913 the Bolshevik paper *Pravda* printed a special six-page edition and set up a holiday committee of textile workers and Bolshevik activists. The day proved a great success: the meeting was in a hall holding 1000 and there was a large overflow. There was such a volume of correspondence from women workers that *Pravda* decided to publish a special paper, *Rabotnitsa* (The Working Woman), though its publication was ended by the outbreak of war the following year. The Bolshevik message of working-class unity and solidarity was expressed by a textile worker: 'The women workers' movement is a tributary flowing into the great river of the proletarian movement and giving it strength.'[32]

Chapter two
Liberation through revolution

DURING THE WAR that broke out in 1914 anger, particularly among working women, mounted over food shortages and spilled over into riots. On 6 April 1915 women in Petrograd smashed up and looted the meat market. In Moscow there were bread riots. By International Women's Day, 23 February 1917, the atmosphere was fully charged. The Petrograd textile women decided to celebrate the day by striking. Neither they nor anyone else knew this was the start of the revolution. How unexpected was the outcome of their action may be gauged by the coldness of the Bolshevik leadership's response to their strike. V Kaiurov, worker leader of the Petrograd District Committee of the Bolshevik Party, expressed his annoyance:

> We learned... of the strike in some textile factories and of the arrival of a number of delegates from the women workers... I was extremely indignant about the behaviour of the strikers, both because they had blatantly ignored the decision of the District Committee of the Party, and also because they had gone on strike after I had appealed to them only the night before to keep cool and disciplined. With reluctance the Bolsheviks agreed to [spreading the strike] and they were followed by other workers—Mensheviks and SRs [Social Revolutionaries]. But once there is a mass strike one must call everybody into the streets and take the lead.[1]

The first Bolshevik leaflet came out on 25 February, two days after the revolution had started.[2] It shows how even a revolutionary leadership can lag. Trotsky describes this beautifully:

the fact is that the February revolution was begun from below, overcoming the resistance of its own revolutionary organisations, the initiative being taken of their own accord by the most oppressed and downtrodden part of the proletariat—the women textile workers, among them no doubt many soldiers' wives. The overgrown bread lines had provided the last stimulus. About 90,000 workers, men and women, were on strike that day... A mass of women, not all of them workers, flocked to the municipal *duma* demanding bread. It was like demanding milk from a he-goat. Red banners appeared in different parts of the city, and inscriptions on them showed that the workers wanted bread, but also not autocracy nor war. Women's Day passed successfully, with enthusiasm and without victims. But what it concealed in itself, no-one had guessed even by nightfall.[3]

If the movement was to succeed the soldiers had to be won over. Here too the women were most prominent, most heroic. Trotsky describes: 'They go up to the cordons more boldly than the men, take hold of the rifles, beseech, almost command: "Put down your bayonets—join us".'[4]

By nightfall on 27 February, the entire Tsarist garrison of 150,000 soldiers had deserted. On the same day the Soviet of Workers' Deputies was formed. On 3 March the Tsar abdicated. *Pravda* cheered:

Hail the women!
Hail the International!
The women were the first to come out on the streets of Petrograd on their Women's Day...
Hail the women![5]

There was tremendous euphoria: contracts, rule books, blacklists were torn up. The women strikers' favourite method was carting the boss out in a wheelbarrow, a magnificent symbolic gesture—the humiliation of the humiliators. For example the director of the Vyborg Spinning Mill tried to explain to a general meeting of workers why he was unable to consider their demand for a wage increase. The women unceremoniously seized him, shoved him in a wheelbarrow and carted him to the canal where, poised perilously on the edge of the bank, he shakily signed a piece of paper agreeing to an increase.[6]

Factory committees were formed and flourished, dominated by skilled, experienced, better-paid workers. The factory committees expressed in microcosm the relationships within the working class at the time. They were elected for six months, subject to recall, but it was the frequently held general meeting which was the sovereign body and had the final say, and the general meeting was not chary about using this power.

The first economic demands of the factory committees were for the eight-hour day, a minimum wage and payment for the days spent toppling the Romanov dynasty. The women in particular were adamant that an eight-hour day should mean eight hours; and in fact the hours fell dramatically, to 7.8 for women and 8.7 for men (including one hour overtime).[7]

This went hand in hand with a strong and growing Bolshevik influence in the factory committees, established early in the munitions industry, later in textiles and other women's industries. In the latter at first most committee members were non-party. For instance, in Skorokhod shoe factory soon after the revolution there were 40 committee members, mostly non-party, but including one woman Bolshevik. At the Kozhevnikov weaving mill the chairperson of the factory committee was a Bolshevik, but the other five women and two men were non-party.[8] This situation changed rapidly. By May the Bolsheviks and their supporters had the hegemony not only in most factory committees, but also on the Petrograd Council of Trade Unions.[9] By September the Bolsheviks were a majority at the first national textile workers' conference.[10]

In all revolutions a workers' leadership tries to unify the working class in order to maximise its strength. A major step in this direction is greatly reducing the wage differentials by disproportionately raising the wages of the low paid, in other words moving towards greater egalitarianism. Women in particular benefit from this. After a rash of strikes in textiles from February to May 1917, skilled workers got a rise of 59 per cent, unskilled 125 per cent. Workers in a Petrograd paper mill succeeded in raising men's wages by 214 per cent, women's by 234 per cent.[11]

Another step in the same direction was the effort of revolutionaries among the skilled workers who built the factory committees to channel women's explosive and violent militancy into the organised labour movement. Socialist women had the same aim, and as early as April 1917, 50 working-class women met to discuss how to organise the women.[12] Also in April, one of Lenin's first acts on returning to Russia was to seek Central Committee support for political work among women.[13]

The results of these efforts, mainly of a few socialists, was astonishing: from practically nothing in February at the time of the revolution, by summer women in textiles, food and other industries were almost completely unionised. In fact they had a higher level of unionisation than the men: in food and textiles women comprised 66 and 69 per cent of the workforce respectively, but trade-union membership stood at about 80 and 70 per cent.[14]

To defend the revolution, factory militias were set up, including women, who served by rota while continuing to work.[15]

Even so the ingrained prejudices of centuries could not be eradicated at a stroke, even by the revolution. As Marx said: 'The tradition of all the dead generations hangs like a nightmare on the brain of the living.'

A prejudice that persisted strongly was male workers' consideration of women workers as backward, badly organised, a drag on the forward march of the class, and hence not fit to represent workers in the leadership of their organisations. Nor were women workers themselves immune from the influence of these prejudices.

Thus women's representation in the leadership of the workers' organisations continued low: of the fifteen on the textile Trade Union Board only two were women. Triangle Rubber, 68 per cent of whose workforce were women, had only two women among the 25 members on the factory committee.[16] In the *soviets*, while women made up half the workforce in Petrograd, on 26-27 March there were 259 women out of 4743 delegates. Examples from other towns tell the same story.[17]

It was still usual for women to be openly discriminated against. At the Pipe Works a woman worker complains: 'Backward workers... cannot imagine a woman as capable of organising the broad masses, and so they make fun of elected representatives of women workers, pointing their fingers as though at a savage and saying with a sneer: "there go our elected representatives".'[18] A worker gave a graphic picture of the difficulties faced by advanced women workers, complaining in the leatherworkers' journal about the behaviour of her male colleagues:

> Instead of supporting, organising and going hand-in-hand with the women, they behave as though we are not equal members of the working family and sometimes do not bother with us at all. When the question of unemployment and redundancies arises, they try to ensure that the men stay and that the women go, hoping that the women will be unable to resist because of their poor organisation and feebleness. When women attempt to speak, in order to point out that the men are behaving wrongly and that we must jointly find a solution, the men will not allow us to speak and will not listen. It is difficult even for the more conscious women to fight against this, the more so since often the mass of women do not understand and do not wish to listen to us.[19]

The fundamental question of equal pay for equal work was never satisfactorily solved by the February revolution. Although there were some women's strikes over the issue and in some factories such as Putilov the low-paid struck and were backed up by delegate meetings of low-paid workers, the male/female differential was so ingrained that equal pay never came about, even though the Bolsheviks fought for it.

As unemployment increased, some factories tried to shift redundancies on to the women.[20] The Bolsheviks fought against this, on the grounds that it would divide the working class,[21] and their influence won increasingly.

As February drew towards October more and more backward sections, including women, did become much better organised as trade unionism spread. In the summer there were strikes of mostly 'backward' women workers in laundries, catering, dye works and such like. They had no tradition or experience, yet got themselves well organised and set up strike committees. Their demands became ever more far-reaching and confident.

As workers' control and workers' confidence strengthened, they felt more and more cheated out of the gains of the revolution, and disillusioned with the Provisional Government: after all the war was still going on, capitalism still continued, inflation rocketed, and every reform had to be struck for.

The October revolution at last installed a government in the interests of the workers and all oppressed humanity. Trotsky said:

> the Revolution is before and above all the awakening of humanity... A revolution does not deserve its name if, with all its might and all the means at its disposal, it does not help the woman—twofold and threefold enslaved as she has been in the past—to get out on the road of individual and social progress.[22]

The task of the Bolsheviks in power was to make this possible, to awaken the vast backward masses and guide them towards running the social order themselves and constructing socialism, according to the popular paraphrase of Lenin's remark: 'Let every cook govern'. As Lenin himself said, the achievements of the revolution needed to be judged by the yardstick that 'the experience of all liberation movements has shown that the success of a revolution depends on how much the women take part in it.'[23]

During the first few days after the revolution a vast number of revolutionary decrees was issued. The great Russian mammoth took a leap from the dark ages to the most advanced social system in the world.

The decrees relating to women during the first year after the October revolution gave them the full right to vote (only Norway and Denmark had that); ended the authority of heads of families; abolished the right of inheritance; established divorce and civil laws making marriage a voluntary relationship; allowed no distinction between legitimate and illegitimate children; gave equal pay (at last!), equal employment rights, paid maternity leave; and dropped adultery, incest and homosexuality from the criminal code. In 1920 free abortion on demand was introduced (it existed nowhere else in the world). In 1923 a commission to study birth control was set up with a number of scientists, and contraceptives were issued by hospitals, maternity homes and women's consultation clinics, and were sold in chemists' shops.

Wide-ranging labour legislation was enacted, starting days after the revolution. For instance on 29 October 1917, four days after the revolution, a decree establishing the eight-hour day was promulgated, and women were banned from working longer. The decree also included wide regulations for the protection of women and juveniles: prohibiting employment in particularly heavy and unhealthy production and in work underground; night work was prohibited and overtime restricted.[24]

The series of decrees was collected and codified in the Labour Code of 1922 which gave life to aspirations for the emancipation of workers in general and women workers in particular. It aimed to encourage women to work in order to raise their status towards independence and equality. Women's liberation was the goal of the Code; the needs of production were secondary to that. The Code was worked out with animated public participation, and backed up by training programmes and welfare. In fact maternity and child welfare provisions in the 1920s were the most advanced in the world at the time. Paid maternity leave was introduced eight weeks before and 8-12 weeks after delivery, also a *layette* benefit of one month's wage and a nursing allowance of a quarter of a month's wage. Breaks for nursing mothers were provided for at least 30 minutes every three and a half hours.[25] This was an astonishing feat of socialist humanitarianism for a country devastated by the First World War and then wracked by civil war.

An order issued by the Commissariat of Labour and the Supreme Economic Council on 14 November 1923 prohibited the employment of women for work consisting *entirely* of carrying or moving loads exceeding 4.1kg. The carrying of loads up to 16.4kg was allowed, but only if it was directly connected with the woman's normal work and if it did not occupy more than one-third of her working day.[26] There was a big body of inspectors to ensure implementation of the protective legislation.

There was also an assault on the family conditions that shackled women. Lenin supported these moves, saying that while women were forced to do all the housework, they would become worn and their talents would be wasted. Not only would they be unable to participate in political activities, they were likely to have no understanding or sympathy with revolutionary ideas.[27] Kollontai insisted that 'separation of kitchen from marriage' is as important in the life of a woman as 'separation of Church from State'. Communal institutions were set up to free women from so-called 'woman's work': maternity homes, nurseries, laundries and mending centres. House communes were set up for single people and married couples, which were superior to private flats. In 1919-20, 90 per cent of Petrograd's population fed communally,

60 per cent of Moscow's—altogether 12 million people.[28]

Prostitution, which had been widespread in Tsarist Russia, disappeared after the revolution. The new moral climate enhanced the dignity of human beings, ousting the degradation of trade in sex; ousted too were the bourgeois with their pocketsful of cash. Prostitutes were now regarded as the victims of class society, not criminals, and great efforts were made to put into action the prevailing idea, as expressed by Lenin: 'return the prostitute to productive work, find her a place in the social economy.' Co-operative workshops were set up for former prostitutes in Moscow, Petrograd and other cities. The women were trained in sewing and other skills. They received medical attention and an intensive campaign was waged against venereal disease.[29]

Besides creating the conditions to awaken and guide women, the Bolsheviks set up an organisational means—Zhenotdel (the Women's Section of the Bolshevik Party), first under Inessa Armand, then Kollontai. It arose out of a highly stimulating and enthusiastic Women's Congress held in November 1918, at which 300 women were expected but which was crowded by 1,147. It was addressed by leading Bolsheviks, including Lenin. Zhenotdel aimed to increase the female membership of the party, only 7.4 per cent in 1920, which reflected the prejudice in the past against women participating in politics, and to draw non-party women into public affairs through delegates' meetings at all levels, from local to national. One of every ten workers and one of every hundred housewives and peasants were each elected by as large a number of women as could be got to participate in the elections. The women thus elected met twice a month under the leadership of a trained party worker and were given a political course.[30]

It was a mammoth task, but Zhenotdel was quite successful, and women did start taking responsibility in all branches of public life. Party membership of women nearly doubled, to 13.1 per cent in 1927.[31] Female trade union membership rose from 1,449,000 in 1923 to 2,569,000 in 1927, when women were 26.1 per cent of the total membership.[32]

The gigantic effort and heroism of the revolution has to be seen in the light of the appalling conditions of the time. In 1920, because of the imperialist attack on the new workers' state—Russia was invaded by foreign armies from all four points of the compass—and the ensuing civil war, industrial production dropped to a mere one-fifth of its 1914 level. The cities shrank, Petrograd in 1920 to a mere 40 per cent of its size at the time of the revolution. Nine million people died of starvation, cold and disease.[33]

Yet the spiritual expansion was astonishing. Of immediate benefit to women was the setting up of 125,000 literacy schools. Many women learnt to read by writing Bolshevik slogans on blackboards.

'The revolution is, in the first place', as Trotsky says, 'an awakening of human personality in the masses—which were supposed to possess no personality.' Respect for the dignity of one's own personality and that of others grew, and factories started passing resolutions to outlaw the swearing and foul language endemic to autocratic Tsarism.[34]

The factories also established Education Commissions, and these put on theatre productions, poetry readings, orchestral concerts. Working men and women flocked to the theatres, ballets, concerts that were previously the preserve of the upper classes. In art it was as if every person picked up a brush and had a go at painting. There was experiment in every field of life. Schools in 1918 opened a month late after the summer break because teachers were thrashing out and organising the new education of the future builders of socialism according to the most up-to-date methods of the most advanced educationists in the world.[35] There was discussion and argument on every street corner about every subject under the sun.

But the Bolsheviks could not hold out. After the failure of revolutions in other countries, resulting in the total isolation of the Russian revolution, the Bolsheviks were forced to introduce the New Economic Policy (NEP) in 1921, which made concessions to the peasantry's aspirations for private gain through free trade.

With the NEP came large-scale unemployment. The unskilled were sacked first, and the women thus hit worst, despite government efforts to protect them—even in 1924 lifting the ban on night work for women to give less excuse for sacking them.

Women's liberation retreated. The communal institutions were run down. In November 1925 it was estimated that only 50,000 communal dinners were served to workers in Leningrad (the renamed Petrograd), 20,000 in Moscow. Only three out of every hundred children had a place in a creche. In conditions of dire poverty freedom of divorce meant that women were 'tied with chains to the ruin of the family hearth'. In 1925 alimony was introduced. Pressure to preserve the traditional family came also from the peasants who wanted to protect their property rights in their farms.[36]

Prostitution too reappeared with private enterprise and increasing unemployment, reaching pre-revolutionary proportions by 1922. In spite of the continued attempt to integrate prostitutes into society by the setting up in the mid-1920s of a network of prophylacteries combining features of VD clinics, workshops and shelters where infected prostitutes were given maintenance, medical treatment, training and eventually job placement, the government fought a losing battle.[37]

Nevertheless, until towards the end of the 1920s the government, in the view even of a Menhevik opponent of the regime, encouraged 'work for women as a means to raise their status. The controlling point of view was women's emancipation rather than labour market policy', and this aim was propagated by 'lively public discussions' about 'increasing the proportion of paid jobs held by women', and assisted to fruition by 'a general and vocational training programme for girls and by expanding welfare institutions which would reduce household work'.[38]

Chapter three
Stalinism

AS WE HAVE SEEN, women in Russia today are once again 'the coolie of the family'. How were they pushed back?

Socialism and women's liberation cannot be built on scarcity. To free working women from their second shift of private family care by social provision demands abundant resources. Russia at the time of the revolution was a backward country, exhausted by three years of world war. Lenin told the Third Congress of Soviets in January 1918:

> The final victory of socialism in a single country is of course impossible. Our contingent of workers and peasants which is upholding Soviet power is one of the contingents of the great world army.[1]

Socialism—and women's liberation—needed the resources that only the workers of the advanced countries could bring. Lenin told the Congress: '...it is the absolute truth that without a German revolution we are doomed.'[2]

Between the élan of the 1917 revolution and the oppression of today revolutionary convulsions did break out in many countries. But they all failed. Russia was left isolated, surrounded by hostile capitalist countries. The working class that had made the revolution with peasant support, numbering only three and a half million in a population of 160 million, largely disappeared into the Red Army that was fighting the civil war, and into the growing bureaucracy; the remnants were almost entirely absorbed into war production. In the circumstances, famine raged and the towns emptied. The peasants, who had loved the Bolsheviks who gave them the land, now turned against the

Communists who took their grain for the Red Army and the towns.

The first step back, the New Economic Policy of 1921, was by force of necessity. Without this concession to the peasants, grain production would have fallen drastically and famine would have become total. But the workers had to pay the price for NEP: unemployment.

> Unemployment delivered a severe blow to attempts at women's liberation, and the economic dependence of women on men got a boost. Oppressive, reactionary trends were strengthened, as the state sought to cut expenditure, and the extensive communal institutions... were run down.[3]

But there is a wide gap between this retreat in the face of necessity and a state policy which consciously subordinates the needs of workers—women and men—to the demands of production and capital accumulation.

Women's best hope for the continuation of revolutionary policies lay with Trotsky's Left Opposition, which proposed to hold the fort and wait for the world revolution—at home by building industry and hence the working class, accompanied by increased workers' democracy, and abroad by striving to extend the revolution. But the Left Opposition was without a strong base in the class which could fight for these policies: that class had been decimated by the civil war.

Stalin, on the other hand, had a base in the party and state bureaucracy. With the decimation of the working class this bureaucracy was left standing above the class; increasingly it was now augmented by the assimilation of former Tsarist bureaucrats whose influence was entirely reactionary, including on working women's issues. From holding power on behalf of the working class, it grew to hold power *over* the working class. Eventually it would become Russia's new ruling class, imposing its policies on those classes below it.

But many battles had yet to be fought. First the bureaucracy, led by Stalin, was able to confront and smash the Left Opposition. Further strengthened, Stalin was then able to smash the Right Opposition of Bukharin and Tomsky, popularly categorised by the slogan 'Kulaks, enrich yourselves'—not inapt for a movement which encouraged the development of private capitalism among the peasantry to solve the state's economic problems (hence of no help to women's advancement).

While a socialist revolution can be achieved only at a single blow, as workers own and control nothing economically and politically unless they own and control the state, a capitalist counter-revolution does not need to seize power all at once, but can extend its tentacles of control in a succession of confrontations with those still adhering to revolutionary traditions. The bureaucracy in the second half of the 1920s already controlled the economy, the police and army. Having now disposed of all credible opposition, Stalin, heading a secure, confident bureaucracy, was poised to culminate his counter-revolution in a massive assault on the peasants through forced collectivisation, and on workers through forced industrialisation.

What this meant for working-class women, who a mere decade earlier had been experimenting with a new liberating life, was total defeat.

With the first Five Year Plan, starting in 1928, all priorities changed almost overnight. Now women were not encouraged to work as a route to emancipation; the government made it almost impossible for them not to—in a rush to accumulate capital through maximum production. The Five Year Plans were designed to make Russia catch up with the West at breakneck speed. Stalin proclaimed in 1931:

> We are fifty or a hundred years behind the advanced countries. We must make good this lag in ten years. Either we do it or they crush us.[4]

This precipitate haste for primitive accumulation, to reach and overtake the advanced countries economically and militarily, constituted the culmination of the Stalinist counter-revolution and the introduction of bureaucratic state capitalism. The priority of the socialist revolution—to direct production as far as possible to the needs of the workers, particularly the women and children—was turned on its head, and the capitalist imperative, as Marx described it, 'Accumulation for accumulation's sake, production for production's sake', became the aim. Consumer goods and services—the key to lightening women's double burden —sank from a high priority to the lowest.

In 1927-28, just before the Five Year Plans, means of production took 32.8 per cent of industrial investment as against

55.7 per cent for consumption. By 1932 means of production was taking 53.3 per cent, from which level it was to rise continuously until it reached 68.8 per cent in 1950.[5] Under this imperative, women's liberation was buried.

The women's organisation Zhenotdel reflected the complete reversal of the government's priorities. It had started in 1919 as the chief campaigner for women's liberation. In 1930 its slogan for International Women's Day, '100 per cent collectivisation!' showed how completely it was now subordinated to the economic aims of the state. Even so, it was abolished in 1932.[6]

Marx and Engels, in whose name Stalinist policy was pursued, had called for special protective regulations for women workers. They had condemned the bourgeois feminists for demanding equal treatment and suggesting that special consideration for women's child-bearing role would weaken women's position at work. Marxists said bourgeois feminists were aiding the capitalists, who opposed any restrictions on conditions of employment. Stalin stood Marx's policy on its head. The ban on underground work for women was lifted in January 1933, acknowledging a *de facto* situation of the previous few years (though the prohibition actually remained on the statute book till October 1940).[7]

In November 1939 the percentage of women among workers in coal mines was 24.8, in iron ore mines 23.6.[8] In a modern automated mine with stringently observed health and safety provisions, there may be a case for equality of opportunity for women who want to become miners. However, simple humanitarian interest can on no account condone women working in the mines in the conditions pertaining in India or other countries in the Western orbit. In Britain, which experienced the industrial revolution earlier than other countries, working men and women fought strenuously for the banning of women and juveniles from labour so damaging to their health.

The Russian mines of the 1930s and 1940s were not modern enterprises: quite the contrary. The hard jobs of coal cutting, digging, shovel work, were hazardous at the best of times. They were much more so after many pits, such as those of the big Donets coal basin in the Ukraine, had been devastated in the Second World War. Yet more than a third of the workers employed in reconstruction of the Donets pits were women. In others they were 50-60 per cent of the workforce.[9]

The value of what protective legislation remained on paper may be judged from the following harrowing story of a woman miner, Tatyana Kreshtopova, in 1937:

> ...I am in the seventh month of pregnancy. In the mine they refuse me the privileges to which I am entitled. It is hard for me to work underground, but I am neither transferred to work above ground nor assigned to easier work. I complained to the division chief, Samsonov, that if the winch doesn't work I have to load stones by hand. 'Never mind, you can stand it,' Samsonov said.
>
> On 26 January, I was transferred: now I run a handcar in the mine gallery, again with Samsonov as chief. Working conditions are even worse. The gallery is very steep; it's tough for me to climb down there, and I suffer from the cold.
>
> I asked Samsonov to let me run a handcar above ground, and he threatened me: 'If you don't want to work in the gallery, I'll fire you as a truant.' I complained to the chairman of the mine committee, Comrade Zarypov; he wrote a note but that didn't help any. My co-workers, the miners Kurmayev and others, reported to Samsonov that it was too hard for me to work underground, particularly on the night shift. Samsonov replied: 'Never mind, she won't have to wait long for her maternity leave.' Another woman in my situation, Astakhova, also ran a handcar underground until the day of her maternity leave.[10]

Trud, the trade union daily, sent a reporter to check the facts. He found them worse than expected: 'It turned out that twelve of the twenty pregnant women employed in the mine were refused their legal privileges'. All this was known to the Public Prosecutor's office, where complaints of women workers had been on file for months, but nothing was being done.[11]

The 1922 Labour Code had guaranteed workers the right to work where they pleased, and to migrate freely. Throughout the 1930s the labour laws were tightened until the whole labour force became a conscripted labour army, tied by internal passports to their place of abode, and tied by workbooks—in which management recorded every detail of their working lives—to their jobs. Freedom to change jobs, to refuse overtime or 'voluntary' rest-day working, night work or shift work were eliminated, with infringements recorded as 'sabotage of the production plan' and punishable by dismissal. Absence for one day without good reason was subject to the same penalty.

By a law of 15 November 1932 dismissal brought automatic eviction from the home which was normally tied to the place of employment, and by a decree of a month later, food supplies and other necessities were put under the control of the factory directors.[12] In 1938 lateness was similarly criminalised. The effect of these decrees is dramatically shown by the following case:

> The defendant Zotova had fallen off the streetcar on her way to work and cut her legs. She reported for work on time, had her name taken down, and announced that she was going to the plant dispensary. There she was given a paper to the effect that medical treatment had been administered and that she had refused a sickness certificate although her condition rendered her unfit for work. The plant management and the judge of the People's Court for the 11th Moscow City district, to whom the evidence concerning Zotova's one-hour absence from work was submitted, found the above-mentioned facts immaterial. The People's Court sentenced Zotova to a four-month term of corrective labour at her place of employment.[13]

The ban on night work for women went the way of the ban on underground work. Night work for women became incorporated into the industrial work pattern when the seven-hour day was introduced in a large number of industries with the first Five Year Plan, in order to make a new three-shift system possible.[14] The new schedules at first involved mostly textile workers, who were predominantly women.

Women's fear of any drop in wages was great when the Five Year Plans were first introduced, as the rise of prices above wages led to a real cut of some 50 per cent in industrial wages.[15] The cost-of-living index was conveniently withdrawn in 1931.[16]

At the same time the intensity of labour was greatly stepped up, the textiles industry, for instance, demanding that four or three looms be tended by each worker where two had been the norm before.[17] Orders from management to work any overtime required to fulfil the Plan were compulsory on pain of dismissal or other punishment. *Trud* reported on 8 May 1934:

> As a rule, every worker does ten overtime shifts a month. Lydia Pankratova, a woman employed in the open-hearth department, worked 49 shifts in February and 34 shifts in March; another woman, Makhnikina, did 47 shifts in February and 34 in March. Nor are these isolated cases.[18]

That is, for Lydia, 49 workdays in a 28-day month!

'Protection of labour'—of the worker's life and health from occupational hazards, with special protection for working women and children and a large body of inspectors to enforce legislation—this had been one of the main objectives of labour policy from the revolution till the Five Year Plans. When maximum production became the guiding principle of all social and economic endeavours, 'protection of labour' became secondary. The accident rate rose alarmingly. In the second quarter of 1928 it was already 35.7 per cent above the fourth quarter of 1927.[19]

To keep control of the workforce in these alienating conditions, the state applied divide and rule tactics. One main prong was bigger wage differentials, accompanied by a campaign against egalitarianism, initiated on 13 June 1931 by 'Comrade Stalin [who] in his historic speech... inflicted a mortal blow on the concept of equal wages in theory and practice, and unmasked with full clarity its anti-Marxist content and practical harmfulness.'[20] A textbook of Soviet labour law in 1939 said: 'Petty bourgeois levelling in the remuneration of labour is socialism's worst enemy. For years levelling has been relentlessly combatted by Marxism-Leninism.' (Today Gorbachev too is as adamantly against egalitarianism, 'levelling-out' as he calls it).

That not unknown Marxist-Leninist, Lenin, not many years previously had done everything in his power to propagate the policy and practice of equal wages for all. In his book **State and Revolution**, two months before the October revolution, he wrote of the aim of

> equality for all members of society in relation to the ownership of the means of production, that is, equality of labour and equality of wages...
> The whole of society will have become a single office and a

single factory, with equality of work and equality of pay.

...technicians, managers and bookkeepers, as well as *all* officials, shall receive salaries no higher than a 'workman's wages'.

After the revolution, in March 1918, Lenin again declared his support 'for the gradual equalisation of *all* wages and salaries in *all* professions and categories'.[21]

Under the Five Year Plans piecework, a form of sweated labour useful to employers for atomising the working class, was the main form of production. Piecework rates quickly diverged so that in September 1931 top rates among industrial workers alone (leaving aside specialists, managers and the intelligentsia) were between four and five times higher than bottom rates.[22] Wage differentiation particularly adversely affected women workers, who mostly could not qualify for higher rates, being concentrated at the lower, unskilled and semi-skilled levels.

The other main prong of the divide and rule tactics was 'socialist competition' or Stakhanovism—named after Alexei Stakhanov, who on 31 August 1935 dug 14 times more coal in one shift than the norm. This dovetailed with differentiated wages. 'The watchwords of socialist emulation', said Alexandra Biryukova, past secretary of the All-Union Central Trade Union Council, 'are greater output, better quality, lower costs.'[23]

Even children were drawn into 'socialist competition'. A top educator said of Young Pioneers, a youth movement embracing nearly all pupils between ten and fifteen: 'The Young Pioneers might be described as the sharp-shooters of socialist competition in the schools.' Their first duty was: 'To set an example of discipline and not permit late-comings or absences; raising attendance and general progress of the pupils to 98 per cent.'[24]

The Stakhanovite movement helped the regime raise performance norms and consequently lower the piecework rates. It thus caused immense hostility among other workers, who correctly looked upon it as a new sweating system and the Stakhanovites as, in English terminology, blacklegs. Many Stakhanovites were attacked, some even murdered. The movement also caused accidents, and some major disasters, especially in the mines.

One reason for the dire conditions of workers in general and women workers in particular was the lack of action from the trade unions in protecting and supporting workers against the impositions of the state and management. The Statute of the Trade Unions now defined the purpose of their activities. It listed as the first objective:

> To organise the socialist competition of workers and officials for the fulfilment and overfulfilment of state plans, for the raising of labour productivity, the improvement in the quality of production, and lowering of its cost.[25]

The unions' zeal in carrying out these tasks was excessive. They insisted on raising performance norms set by the plant. They even used the courts to prevent wage rises above official limits.

On egalitarianism, the trade union position was given by the 1941 Plenary Session of the All-Union Central Trade Union Council, which 'imposed on all trade union organisations the obligation to struggle for the complete elimination of the rotten practice of equal wages,'[26] often called 'the equality racket'. This helped keep low wages, where women predominated, even lower.

Child care is perhaps the most crucial determinant of freedom for women to develop their abilities. For the early Bolsheviks creches and kindergartens were in the party programme as early as 1903. The German revolutionary Klara Zetkin equated women's emancipation with women being in paid employment with household duties (cooking, cleaning, child care) transferred to public institutions, so women could be free to make use of their talents.[27] The June 1936 decree on the family, however, looked to a big increase in child care institutions for a different priority: to remove, as the People's Commissariat said in 1930, 'the chief obstacle to the mass absorption of women into production'.[28]

In the the early years of the Soviet regime social insurance had been the mainstay of the government's social policy. It had one indisputable aim: to give security to wage and salary earners by insuring them against all the hazards threatening their ability to earn a living. As we have seen, health and maternity insurance was so widely developed that in some respects it outdid the best provision elsewhere in the world[29]—and that when Russia was almost the poorest country in Europe. After 1933 social insurance too was administered by the trade unions. Its aim then became the same as theirs:

The task of social insurance lies in the many-sided, unremitting daily struggle for increasing the yield of labour... This is a point of honour for social insurance agencies, for all social insurance officers. This is their foremost duty, and by its execution their performance will have to be judged.[30]

Even maternity benefits were slashed. In the 1920s eligibility for maternity benefits, which were then equal to the full wage, applied to all women. This changed to eligibility for the full wage only if the woman was employed for the three preceding years, including two at the last job, and then only if she was a union member. Women 'shock workers' and technicians had better conditions, non-union workers worse. The period of payment, previously eight weeks before and 8-12 weeks after delivery, was cut in 1938 to five weeks before and four weeks after.[31]

Working conditions under Stalinism constituted a monstrous burden for men. For women they were all but intolerable, since they had once again to carry alone the double burden the October revolution had so spiritedly fought to relieve them of. With economic priority given to heavy industry as against consumer goods and services, working women's lives were grim indeed.

To buttress the regime's new aims a new ideology was needed. In the social sphere relations needed to be created that would enhance the effort to extract maximum surplus value out of the maximum number of workers. This required the stabilising and disciplining of a workforce largely unused to factory conditions and very volatile, having gone through the huge upheavals of rapid collectivisation and industrialisation—leading to large population movements, vast numbers of abandoned children, and other traumas. It further required the raising of the birth rate to provide more factory fodder, and the clipping of the wings of the new youth that had grown up in condiitons of cultural, social and sexual freedom: sexual freedom was now to be castigated as anti-Marxist 'sexual debauchery' or 'anarchy' and sex kept strictly for marriage.[32] Capitalist reaction has always turned to glorification of the family to enhance its hold, and the new bureaucratic state capitalist reaction in Russia was no different, except that the *paean* was sung in the names of Marx, Engels, Lenin and Stalin.

The new thinking was codified in a decree of 27 June 1936

called 'In Defence of Mother and Child', and its provisions were strengthened in 1944. It reversed all the gains of the revolution in respect of family law and reintroduced Tsarist prejudices and restrictions. It propagated a cult of the family, tightened up marriage procedures, ending recognition of *de facto* marriages and reintroducing the notions of promiscuity, adultery and illegitimacy of children, put divorce beyond the means of workers' families, compelled parents to take responsibility for their children's education and behaviour, introduced alimony, banned abortion, extolled motherhood and aimed to increase child care facilities. Male homosexuality had been criminalised two years earlier with penalties of from three to eight years imprisonment.

Stalin's cult of the family served his wider purpose in many ways. As in all capitalist regimes, the family was seen as the cheapest institution for the nourishment and care of the present generation of workers, and also for the bearing and rearing of the next. Or as Kate Millett put it: 'Stalin's Russia preferred to bolster the family to perform the functions the state had promised but did not choose to afford.'[33] Equally compelling, however, as Trotsky remarks, was 'the need of the bureaucracy for a stable hierarchy of relations, and for the disciplining of youth by means of 40,000,000 points of support for authority and power.'[34]

The most drastic clause in the decree concerned the total banning of abortion (except for danger to life and hereditary diseases) which was trumpeted by a huge campaign of acclamation accompanied by total silence on the question of contraception (which became very scarce after the decree).[35] To reach and outstrip the West, manpower was needed. The looming clouds of war added urgency. Two women apologists for the government stated plainly that abortion 'not only harms women's health, but also undermines the interests of the state'.[36]

Stalin was more crude: 'We need men. Abortion which destroys life is not acceptable in our country.'[37]

The decree did not stop abortions. The numbers had been falling when it was legal before 1936,[38] but they rose sharply in 1938, then by 150 per cent between 1939 and 1948 in the RSFSR.[39] Nor did it succeed in raising the birth rate, which rose briefly to 38.3 per 1000 population in 1938,[40] but then fell to 31.2 per thousand in 1940 and continued to go down.

What the decree against abortion did lead to was deaths from the consequences of 'incomplete abortions', which in 1938-39 accounted for 12.7 deaths for every 100,000 women in the towns. It also led to infanticide, a practice that had declined after the revolution, but increased, together with abandonment of children, after the decree.[41]

A further effort to stop abortion and raise the birthrate was the extolling of the 'joys of motherhood', the 'blessings of motherhood', which covered many columns of print. Abundant motherhood was rewarded with decorations and differential monetary grants: Motherhood Medal First and Second Class for those with five or six children; Motherhood Glory First, Second and Third Class for those with seven, eight or nine children; Heroine Mother for those with ten. A special tax was introduced for single citizens and small families.[42] The financial rewards were miserly, no benefit being given for fewer than six children and benefit ending when the child was five years old. The government claimed the 1936 decree 'In Defence of Mother and Child' helped Soviet women realise full equality with men. Trotsky called it 'a law against women'. How tragically right he was!

The 'woman question', much to the fore in the early days of the revolution, disappeared. Between 1917 and 1930 there were 301 entries in resolutions and decrees. This dropped to three between 1930 and 1967.[43]

Prostitution likewise disappeared from public view, though it continued rife throughout the period. Trotsky reports a sudden *Izvestia* news item of autumn 1935 on the arrest in Moscow of 'as many as a thousand women who were secretly selling themselves on the streets of the proletarian capital.'[44]

If social advance can be gauged by the condition of women, so can social retreat. Trotsky sums this up well: '...the consecutive changes in the approach to the problem of the family in the Soviet Union best of all characterise the actual nature of Soviet society and the evolution of its ruling stratum.'[45]

The years immediately after the socialist revolution of 1917 brought women nearer to liberation than before or since. The counter-revolution, of which the changes Trotsky talked of were part, created in Russia—and later in Eastern Europe—a new state capitalist class society. Today women in Russia are oppressed because, like women in the West, they are subjected to the same double burden that is imposed by a capitalist society.

Chapter four

What does perestroika offer?

GORBACHEV is attempting to reform the Russian economy through *perestroika*, 'restructuring'. To rally the population around it, he introduced *glasnost*, 'openness', which has been widely taken up to expose hitherto unrevealed aspects of Russian life. This includes the position of women in society, as we have seen. But what do the attempted reforms offer women?

To answer this question we may assess some of the changes that have been made so far, but, more important, we must examine the reasons *why* reforms are being proposed.

Stalin's dehumanising primitive capitalist accumulation had one aim in mind—to lift the Russian economy by its bootstraps to the level of the advanced capitalist countries as quickly as possible. It certainly achieved spectacular results, comparable with Japan, Korea, Brazil or Hong Kong, and on a much larger scale. It raised the Russian economy to the second largest in the world, well protected by a powerful military machine.

Three main factors enabled the Russian economy, rich in natural resources, to achieve dynamic growth under Stalin: the influx of the peasantry into industry, the drawing of nearly all women into production, and a high birthrate. Despite the harsh working conditions, social unrest was muted, partly because of the totalitarian terror which consigned millions to slave labour camps, but also because of the rapid upward mobility offered by the expanding economy. The newly arrived raw peasant became an unskilled worker, but could soon ascend the escalator to become a skilled worker, a foreman, a director. Personal solutions to dissatisfaction in a developing backward economy can supercede social solutions, particularly under a dictatorship.

But the escalator slows down as the sources of the dynamism dry up. There is now a shortage of labour in Russian agriculture, the pool of potential female labour is dry, and the birth-rate has slumped. The path of extensive expansion is closed. In addition the burden of armaments has become more and more of a drag on the economy. The fact that Moscow aims at military parity with Washington, when the national income of the Warsaw Pact countries is only a quarter of that of the NATO countries, means that military competition is crippling Russian economic development.

Further expansion can come only from higher productivity through the more intensive use of labour and natural resources.

However, the turn to higher productivity is beset by obstacles emanating from the economic stranglehold of a conservative and corrupt bureaucracy—a huge lag in advanced technology outside the military sphere, a sceptical, not committed, workforce, and other brakes on development. With the totalitarian terror also necessarily removed (because it was becoming economically counter-productive) there is now every encouragement to seek collective social solutions.

Eastern Europe furnishes a graphic illustration of the connection between economic development and social strife under a state capitalist regime. Strikes and demonstrations have occurred in all the more developed countries, starting with the most highly developed, East Germany in 1953, then in Hungary, Poland, Czechoslovakia, at a time when the more backward countries, including Russia, remained largely dormant.

Now Russia is the second largest economy in the world, the social escalator is at a standstill, and the pace of economic growth is slow. This situation has already given rise to collective protest on a mass scale, taking first a nationalist form, then breaking out in powerful strikes.

Gorbachev knows he is sitting on a powder keg. To date the economic dynamism has delivered an economy markedly distorted towards armaments and producer goods. The fact that it is centrally owned and controlled not by the working class to satisfy the needs of all, but by a bureaucratic state capitalist class bent on accumulation to compete with the West, has enabled it, even more thoroughly than free market economies, to hold down the production of consumer goods and services. This has bred both a smouldering resentment against the culpable authorities, the bureaucrats, and a deeply ingrained alienation from the production process.

For Gorbachev it is urgent to change these attitudes. *Glasnost* and *perestroika* are to rally the people against the entrenched, conservative bureaucracy who are unprepared or unable to move from the command economy which has led to the present *impasse*. The aim is a situation where workers take initiatives and responsibility for their work in self-financing enterprises, and to overcome the inadequate supply of consumer goods and services. If *perestroika* is to bring *any* benefit, particularly to women, then consumer goods and services are central, for it is here that women's double burden is at its heaviest and here that the regime has consistently failed them.

Currently food in state shops may be in short supply but it is cheap; prices for some basic foods have not changed for 20 years, hence food uses up 15 per cent of the state budget in subsidies. For *perestroika* to succeed it requires a rational cost accounting system; this would considerably raise the prices of basic foods. This is a risky undertaking, liable to lead to social convulsions as price rises did in Poland, especially as expenditure on food, because of much lower wages, takes up a far bigger chunk of people's income in Russia (close to half) than in Western countries (under one-fifth in the USA). Understandably Gorbachev does not want Gdansk to come to Minsk or Pinsk.[1] So the only change to come about so far is that the Agro-Industrial Committee bureaucracy has 'swelled excessively' but done 'nothing in practice to improve the supply of foodstuffs.'[2]

In his walkabouts Gorbachev was made very aware of another source of disaffection: the new co-operatives (in reality small-scale private enterprises) that he is heavily promoting. 'The shops are empty', someone interrupts him to remark, 'and where do co-operatives get their meat from? They buy state meat and then sell it in co-operatives!' Many voices vent their frustration: 'There is everything there... But what prices one has to pay there.'[3]

Indeed so! A kilo of meat in a state shop costs 1.8 rubles when available after queueing, while a kilo of veal in the private market, where it is available without queueing, is ten rubles—an average day's pay.[4]

Financial autonomy of enterprises, to try to make them more

competitive—a major plank of *perestroika*—was introduced in stages till by the beginning of 1989 it was universal. Instead of improving matters, as had been hoped, the situation has deteriorated. A *Pravda* correspondent commented: 'Muscovites assess the progress of restructuring in terms of the goods in the stores. But at the height of the harvest we could not organise normal working. We speak in the new way but we work in the old way. We cannot tolerate that any longer.'[5]

A metalworker delegate to the 19th Party Conference in June 1988 tried

> to bring home to delegates the pain which is troubling workers and all people... The workers are asking bluntly: Where is the restructuring? The situation concerning food supplies in the shops is as poor as it was before. Furthermore, sugar rationing has been introduced. There was no meat before and there is none now. And as for consumer goods, they seem to have disappeared altogether.[6]

The situation causes extreme embarrassment and anxiety to top government officials. *Pravda* reports on their crisis meeting over Moscow fruit and vegetable supplies: 'Delay in solving the problem of supplying the market with high-quality foodstuffs is developing into an acute social and political problem—that was the stern judgment of the prevailing situation.'[7]

Top economists have predicted inevitable social and political unrest after a period of one-and-a-half to two years unless there is fast radical reform which would give a quick boost to living standards.[8] This is an ominous situation for Gorbachev. The ghost of his predecessor Khrushchev lurks in the background. In the late 1950s and early 1960s Khrushchev tried, like Gorbachev, to introduce reforms and bring the high-ranking embezzlers and bribe-takers to book. Someone who remembered the time wrote to *Izvestia*:

> The response was that shops throughout the country stopped selling basic necessities and other goods. This was partially due to the poor harvest and other objective factors, but I believe that this was also helped by economic sabotage designed to make the people dissatisfied with the leader of the day. Those dark forces got their way. Within one week

of N S Khrushchev's removal, everything appeared in the shops again—as if by magic! For a time, at least.[9]

Glasnost, riots and strikes have forced the authorities to alleviate the social situation—not by building more or improving existing buildings—but by turning over some of the luxury buildings and prestige projects to public service. Gorbachev took the initiative on his visit to Krasnoyarsk Kray in Siberia. After the hammering he got on his walkabout from the people over the state of welfare, he persuaded the local party leaders to hand over their newly built headquarters to the health service, and themselves to stay in their old building.[10] Riots in Alma Ata, capital of Kazakhstan, got the luxury dachas of party leaders, built at party expense, hastily confiscated and given over to hospitals, children's homes and hostels with places for 2,000 people.[11]

Gorbachev walks a tightrope. He wants to loosen the stifling hold of the conservative bureaucracy, but without opening the door to massive social upheaval. If the authority of the bureaucracy is to be weakened, then other ideological authorities must be strengthened. The family and religion are two which directly affect the lives of women.

In his book **Perestroika: New Thinking for our Country and the World**, published in 1987, Gorbachev leads the way, stressing all the traditional bourgeois values of the family and woman's place in it:

women no longer have enough time to perform their everyday duties at home—housework, the upbringing of children and the creation of a good family atmosphere. We have discovered that many of our problems—in children's and young people's behaviour, in our morals, culture and in production—are partially caused by the weakening of family ties and slack attitudes to family responsibilities... We are holding heated debates, in the press, in public organisations, at work and at home, to put the question of what we should do to make it possible for women to return to their purely womanly mission.

Press, radio and television follow, increasingly often expressing the opinion that women are losing their 'characteristic qualities' because of being overworked in the job and the home;

that they have no time to bring up their children, which is why there is strife in the family and the number of divorces is increasing. The conclusion drawn from this is that women should return to the home. Women themselves—80 per cent in a poll taken—say No! when asked if they would leave work if their family were fully provided for.[12] Their preference, however, does not address the government's social and economic problem, hence does not count.

The big increase in juvenile drunkenness, crime, psychological disturbance, absconding from home, child abuse and so on, is laid firmly at the door of the inadequate family. The solution? Enforce the laws designed to strengthen the family and increase parental responsibility for the care of their children.[13] This is essential, **Pravda** claims, as 'a complete personality cannot develop outside the family, and... the foundations of physical and mental health are laid in the family and nowhere else.'[14]

Incidentally, in Estonia the new People's Front which formed during the national upsurge of 1988 also idealises the family, declaring in its draft programme: 'Once again the position of the family has to be raised in esteem and to be recognised as being equal to other chief institutions in society.'[15]

Compare this with the attitude to the family of the Bolsheviks in power, when, to liberate women, the utmost efforts were made to create the material conditions for the take-over by society of the family's functions—and abolish women's domestic slavery. The current propaganda in countries East and West glorifying the family, and women's central role in it, stabs at the very heart of the effort at women's liberation.

This emphasis on a woman's place being in the home also serves the current needs of the Russian economy. *Perestroika* is intended to rationalise the economy, making it leaner and fitter; the shake-out of labour is expected to be more than ten million and possibly up to 16 million people by the year 2000. At the same time the government is unhappy about the higher birthrate among Russia's Moslems—nearly four times the average. So it wants to raise the birthrate among European Russians. Raising the birthrate and rationalising production can be secured at one blow—get women out of the workforce and having babies (but in European Russia only; in the Asian republics the stress is on production, not reproduction).

The most direct approach to the problem is to prolong maternity leave. In 1981-83 women received the right to partially paid leave from work for up to one year, and unpaid leave up to one and a half years. Four women in five took the one year, and there was a rapid rise in births. In the cities the number of families with two and three children is increasing.[16] In addition some part-time working was allowed, lighter work for pregnant women and women with children under one and a half years old, and home work if the woman was on leave to care for a sick child, with retention of pay.

In Estonia, where small families are particularly common, additional measures are being taken. Notices in shops inform women with several children or children under the age of three to go to the head of the queue, there is an increase in children's goods in shops, and second-hand clothes shops are appearing. In 1989, 5 per cent of housing is reserved for young families, who were also to receive advantages in the allocations from housing co-operatives.[17] Efforts are also being made to extend kindergarten facilities.

However, as Pukhova, chairman of the Committee of Soviet Women, remarked at the 19th Party Conference:

> Each of the recent Five Year Plans has been marked by new benefits for women. Maternity and child welfare has been raised to the level of state policy. But have all these ideas been implemented? Not in the least![18]

Gorbachev was given a nice illustration of this point on his walkabout in Siberia, where the following conversation took place:

> *Gorbachev*: We are thinking not of ourselves only but of children too, how they will be...
> *Woman*: People have to wait ten years to get a place in a kindergarten. My son had already started his school education when a notice came about a vacancy in the kindergarten!
> *Gorbachev*: Well, I will tell you that is shameful.
> Woman: Whose shame? It is not our shame but that of our leading comrades.[19]

The demands of the miners who struck in July 1989 also justified Pukhova's scepticism. They sought redress for women who worked in hazardous coal-mining operations: a wage increase of up to 60 per cent—double the all-round increase—as well as an additional six days leave, and maternity leave of three years at the woman's full average wage.[20]

The new economic structures, such as the team contract, often work against women's interests. The needs of women with children, for instance, conflict with the greater competitiveness to complete the Plan that perestroika brings in its wake. If they try to exercise their rights, they come into conflict with the administration, the work collective of the shop or team, and become an unwanted workforce. When staff cuts are made, women are the first to be sacked.[21]

In other ways the changes simply look better than they really are. Since the advent of perestroika some ministries concerned with the manufacture of heavy machinery are withdrawing women from night work—but at a pace which will take more than fifty years to complete![22]

Religion too is getting a helping hand from the state.

The state and religion were separated after the revolution, religion becoming a purely private matter, with no institutional status. The official attitude is atheism, with propaganda supposed to be carried out on its behalf. Now, however, the state is pandering to religion and the church in order to bolster the ideology that it wants to prevail, mop up the numerous frustrations and yearnings, and even help out in the inadequate social sector with charitable works. It is returning monasteries and relics to the church in televised ceremonies,[23] printing bibles (53,000 in Georgia alone), religious calendars (10,000 more than before in the same republic), and three or four times more new theological publications, despite the paper shortage.[24] For the first time ever, in August 1988 the Metropolitan church leader of Leningrad and Novgorod, Tallinn diocese, visited the Eastonian Communist Party Central Committee.[25]

At the celebrations for the millenium of the Russian Orthodox Church in mid-1988, Anton Gromyko, the USSR president, stated:

The Soviet leadership welcomes the participation of the multinational Russian church and other religious organisations of our country in active efforts that meet the lofty criteria of Soviet patriotism...[26]

Some weeks later the church was granted legal status.[27]

With the church leading millions of followers and *perestroika* entering the rapids, the state needs *rapprochement* to help prop it up. It requires the church to act as a conservative force holding back current and potential social protest.

The *Catholicos* of all Armenians—whose church is ever loyal to the government—lived up to expectations admirably during the strikes and demonstrations connected with the national uprising in the region in 1988. He supported peaceful demonstrations unconnected with strikes. But when the ferment deepened into widespread strikes throughout the country, the *Catholicos* changed his tune, calling for

> mutual respect and confidence between the leadership and the state and the citizens within the law—this is true patriotism and the benign imperative... Disorderly and unbalanced acts... constitute a deviation from the correct path... Promise to support me and to use every means to bar the way to hasty action. Promise to remain peaceful and tranquil, peaceful and undisturbed. Promise to devote yourself to your daily work, in discipline and conscious of your obligations.

He therefore wished to

> express my satisfaction that in these recent months Soviet armed forces have stood guard over the sons and daughters of our people.[28]

Gorbachev has learned well the lesson of Poland, where the Catholic Church provided both a focus and a brake for the militancy of Solidarity.

As we have seen, one of the biggest problems caused by an entrenched bureaucracy is corruption. This has been greatest in the sphere of housing. *Glasnost* and *perestroika*, exposing some of the corruption, is forcing the release of some grand buildings for social purposes. This is an easy target. A few bureaucrats fall, but without threatening the collective interests of the bureaucracy as a whole, while the results—additional buildings for hospitals and kindergartens—are there for all people to see, and at no extra cost to the state.

In 1982 Soviet leader Leonid Brezhnev visited Azerbaijan. A mansion was specially built in Baku, the capital, for his brief stay. It then remained empty until June 1988 (and *glasnost*), when it was converted to a wedding palace.[29] Other sumptuous guest houses, one a complex of buildings in a magnificent park in Baku, were handed over to the Ministry of Health. The grand scale of these guest houses may be judged by the fact that some handed over in Turkmenia now hold 1,700 hospital beds and provide kindergarten and Young Pioneer accommodation for 1,200 children.

These handovers are of undoubted benefit to working-class women and give a glimpse of the possibilities for alleviating the pressure that inadequate consumer services force on women, through the elimination of the bureaucrats' greed and corruption alone—even without changing economic priorities towards the satisfaction of workers' needs. Rallying the people around *perestroika*, however, comes up against the ingrained habits of a bureaucracy that, in an unequal society, demands its privileges. An example from Kazakhstan illustrates this. There a number of towns operated 'small hotels' reserved exclusively for especially important guests. These comfortable private hotels were, as a rule, built with funds allocated for the construction of housing, hospitals and kindergartens—all of which are in acute short supply in the republic.

> When Kazakhstan's new leadership undertook to restore the republic's moral climate, more than 700 private residences, hotels and 'hunting lodges' were converted into housing for needy families and into polyclinics, sanatoriums, Young Pioneer camps and dormitories. Amid much fanfare, the luxurious 'small hotel' in Arkalyk was turned over to the Turga Bauxite Mining Adminstration, which turned it into a sanatorium for its employees.
>
> Just six months later, however, the miners werre evicted from the building, which reverted to its former status. Now the hotel is being redecorated to suit the tastes of its high-ranking guests, with brand-new furniture and carpeting, an expensive sound system and magnificent baths.

One of the evicted miners remarked: 'I think the province leaders grew tired of playing at restructuring. Now everything is going back to the way it used to be.'[30]

Contradictions of this sort abound in the attempt to promote *perestroika* by beating down corruption. In the absence of workers' power, no matter how often the corruption is scotched, it will breed afresh, as it does in all capitalist countries.

Gorbachev, as always, is caught in a dilemma. He wants the conservative bureaucracy to be shaken by popular pressure but not to the extent of destabilising it critically, let alone eliminating it; and he comes to its defence. Simplistically he quotes an *average* salary for *all* party workers of 216 rubles per month, and an *average* wage for the country of 203 rubles, and, hiding behind these totally unreal averages, asks: 'What is that, a discrepancy? No, comrades!' And, he goes on, 'in the whole country there are 850 party cars—850 for the whole country!' Yet while he tries to wriggle out of embarrassment over accusations levelled at bureaucratic corruption, he argues strongly against moves towards greater equality in pay and instead for a differential incentive pay structure: 'Levelling out has corrupted people,' he says.[31]

'Levelling out', or moves towards egalitarianism, as we have seen, is a strong feature of all revolutionary workers' movements; it serves to unify the working class in struggle. The decrease of wage differentials was energetically pursued by the Russian revolution of 1917 with the enthusiastic backing of the Bolshevik leaders. One of the prime aims of movements towards egalitarianism is to close the gap between the pay of women, who form the major proportion of lower-paid unskilled workers, and men. The capitalist class, on the other hand, constantly fights against decreasing differentials, in order to atomise the working class and maintain control over it; they also enable more surplus value to be extracted from workers. The capitalist class thus prefers differential wage incentive schemes.

Stalin waged an unremitting war against egalitarianism during his state-capitalist counter-revolution, thus pushing back women's equality. Gorbachev continues this tradition, consistently arguing against 'levelling out' and in favour of incentive schemes. These form a big part of his campaign for financial autonomy and greater competition under *perestroika*.

Reforms from above, made for, rather than by, the people, enter into a quagmire of contradictions, often leading to the opposite outcome to that intended. For example, to bypass and weaken the bureaucracy and propagate the ideas of *perestroika*, the authorities have set up various societies, but, as Gorbachev was informed, 'bureaucratic apparatuses have emerged in them... to such an extent that we have ended up with something different from what we wanted.' Gorbachev already knew all about this and elaborated:

> And their first concern is for a direct government telephone line, good premises, a car and so forth. And workers in the localities, so that they have someone to give instructions to. Often this is as far as the activity of social organisation goes... This is a widespread phenomenon. Many people are pursuing their own selfish interests, but want to promote them in the convenient guise of concern for the people and socialism.[32]

Is this not the hypocrisy of the 'national interest' practised by all ruling classes?

Another example of 'ending up with something different from what we wanted' is the attempt to get rid of shoddy goods by quality control. The result is fewer goods on the shelves. The irrational accounting system sees to that. A detailed item-by-item cost accounting system would cause the prices of basics, now cheap, to rocket. Cost accounting—basic to restructuring—has therefore to be postponed, for three or four years says Aganbegyan, the top economist; more likely indefinitely, while consumer goods and services fail to catch up with needs.

The result is that Gorbachev and the reformers are caught in a trap from which there is no escape, and it leads constantly to contradictory actions: lifting the lid on restrictions, then closing it when collective protest gets out of hand; fulminating against corruption among the bureaucracy, but not eradicating it because that would be too destabilising; encouraging private enterprise and co-operatives, then curtailing their area of activity because they lead to inflation; and so on and so on.

This zigzagging essentially preserves the *status quo*, but fuels the disillusionment and anger. This was substantiated in a discussion with the editorial board of **Novy Mir** in mid-1988. Vasiliy Selyunin, a contributor, stated:

there have been no changes in the economic mechanism in 1988... I do not think we should expect any results from the new system in 1988, for the very simple reason that there is nothing new in this system. Just as, before, all production was planned from above, so it is being planned in 1988. The only thing is a new word has appeared: state orders.[33]

Self-financing is intended to encourage horizontal trade in place of state orders and supplies. But the difficulty of acquiring scarce suplies forces directors to decide that they are 'in favour of having all [their] output—all 100 per cent—produced on the basis of state orders'; this is 'at least some guarantee that for their production the necessary resources will be allocated' by the state.[34] So, as Selyunin continues:

> Just as the entire output was distributed via stocks and supply orders—I mean the output of industrial goods—so is it now being distributed. There has been no change here. And there can be no change. If it is all planned, then you have to tell us for whom the output is intended. So there is simply no place for free wholesale trade. Just as the prices were fixed above for output, so they are fixed now. And so on and so forth. And so, when the top button is done up correctly, the whole of the shirt is fastened lop-sided.

He looks at the future of *perestroika*:

> The concept of the 13th Five Year PLan is now being drawn up... As yet, all the ideas that are being built into the concept are old. And so, as before, there is planning of output by injunction, with all the consequences of this.
> So there will not be any place for economic reform in the next Five Year Plan either.[35]

The result is eloquently described by another well-known writer, Aleksander Adamovich:

> We are all witnesses of how the ministerial bureaucracy has very skilfully not buried economic reform, but managed to paralyse and castrate it. By doing this it managed not merely to put the brakes on our economy but to discredit to a certain degree restructuring itself, because precisely this makes it impossible for restructuring to give our population the fruits

which would already be felt and thus, so to speak, activate support for restructuring.[36]

This is not a forecast for the future only, but a situation that has already developed. With the state planning as before, ordering as before, supplying as before, the bureaucracy consequently right in the centre as before, 'the command apparatus is still very great,' comments **Pravda**. 'It produces nothing but paper. Everyone writes, orders, and issues directives,'[37] reducing economic independence to nothing.[38]

Perestroika, which involves self-financing, in the final analysis clashes with the Five Year Plan and its accompanying centralised price-fixing and supplies.

So Gorbachev's accession to office and attempts at reforms have coincided not with higher standards of living and the relaxation of women's oppressive double burden, but rather the opposite. The disappointment is profound and the hostility to the bureaucracy and suspicion of its every move pervasive.

A conversation held by Gorbachev with workers at Krasnoyarsk Kray in September 1988 speaks volumes:

[Video: Gorbachev and Raisa Gorbacheva in crowd shouting out comments].

[Man] Nothing, there's nothing, you cannot even have a wash here if you want to.

[Gorbachev] And this is in the region where there is the most water.

[Woman] But not hot water!

[Man] So it's probably the region where there are the most complaints, then! [Further indistinct comments about water from the crowd].

[Gorbachev] ...tens of billions of rubles have been directed here for over 12 years, tens of billions of rubles to one *kray*. And it turns out that the proportion...

[Voice] But there has been no return on it.

[Gorbachev] I'll make it all clear when I get going. If you take a look, then it turns out that the proportion of the money that is directed to housing, to schools, to facilities for children is less than in other regions. And that is in Siberia, where a new region is being opened up. It is not right. We have to put it right. And I can see that what you keep saying, as it happens, comes to... [interrupted by question from crowd] Eh?

[Man] It won't happen.

[Gorbachev] What won't happen?

[Man] What you are talking about won't happen.

[Gorbachev] Things being put right, you mean?

[Man] Do you think it is me alone?

[Gorbachev] ...where there is rapid development of natural riches... where there is construction... social development is lagging behind... And that is not tolerable. Now, the way it has turned out is that the capacities have been built, but who is to work them? We need people, without people and facilities for them, we'll get nowhere.

[Man] So it is we who are to blame?

[Gorbachev] No, no, no.

[Man] Of course not.

[Gorbachev] No, you cannot be blamed for this... it is the centre which is to blame, the planning bodies and the ministries. That is, they wanted to grab the capacities as soon as possible, to make their report and say they had done their bit, but what are we to do with these capacities if there are no people? That's a dead affair.

[Man] Mikhail Sergeyevich, will they show everything on television, or will they cut half of it out? Tell us honestly.

[Gorbachev] All of it, all of it.

[Man] No, only topical issues, of course, this is what I mean.

[Gorbachev] They will show it.

[Man] Will they show the topical ones?[39]

The alienation from state-directed production could not be more clearly stated than by another person in Krasnoyarsk Kray, a once rich agricultural area now short of food, speaking to Gorbachev three years after the start of his reforms, who tells of private farms 'where the peasant keeps five or six head of cattle... his wife works as a milkmaid and herdswoman,' and they make a handsome profit. 'Why is he going to the [state] farm to work? He is going there in order to steal, to support his farm.' 'Right,' answers Gorbachev.[40]

Izvestia's postbag reads: 'Restructuring has given us nothing!' 'The people are tired of waiting!' These feelings, says the paper, 'are growing stronger.'[41]

Izvestia comments: 'Unless forceful steps are taken to correct this situation today, tomorrow we may find ourselves talking about the restructuring in the past tense.'[42]

In the short term, therefore, *perestroika* brings working women a heavier daily burden, it provides fewer consumer goods, and keeps services such as housing, public health and child care residual. In the long term it promises unemployment, largely for women, and especially pregnant women and those with children. Accompanying the economic hardship will be the ideological baggage of the strong family and women's 'irreplaceable' role in it: bearing the children, rearing them, caring for them and the husband, and doing all the domestic work—being, in Trotsky's words, 'the coolie of the family'.

Gorbachev will not be able to turn the economy round, first because of the contradictions which each reform leads to; secondly because of the government's priorities will continue to be accumulation for profit, not consumption for need.

Whatever the scenario, women's liberation has no place. This can only be achieved by overturning the state capitalist class and introducing socialism under the control of the workers. Russia today has a massive working class of well over a hundred million people. Half of these are women. Doubly oppressed, alienated, deeply resentful of bureaucratic state control, they will be ready, when their confidence is rebuilt, to 'storm the heavens' as they did so grandly in the past. A triumphant working class would take up where Stalin's counter-revolution forced the Bolsheviks to leave off, introducing, with far more advanced technical resources, all the material conditions for off-loading from women's shoulders the yoke of their double burden. Only then will women be truly equal and free.

Notes

Introduction

1. H Scott, **Women and Socialism: Experiences from Eastern Europe** (London 1976), page 209
2. M Buckley, 'Soviet Interpretations of the Woman Question' in B Holland (editor) **Soviet Sisterhood** (London 1985) pages 24 and 50
3. L Trotsky, **Women and the Family** (New York 1984) page 42
4. L Trotsky, **Problems of Everyday Life** (New York 1973) page 65
5. K Marx, **Capital**, volume 1 (London 1977) page 652

PART ONE: WOMEN IN RUSSIA TODAY
Chapter 1: WOMEN AND WORK

1. Holland, page 119
2. Holland, pages 119-20; A Heitlinger, **Women and State Socialism** (London 1979) page 99
3. Holland, page 12; **Militant International Review** (herafter referred to as **MIR**), number 38, Autumn 1988
4. Speech by Z P Pukhova, chairman of the Committee of Soviet Women, at 19th CPSU Conference, in *Pravda*, 2 July 1988, translated in BBC, **Summary of World Broadcasts** (hereafter referred to as **SWB**), SU/0199, 9 July 1988
5. **MIR**, number 38.
6. **The Guardian**, 23 January 1988
7. **The Guardian**, 23 January 1988
8. *Ogonyok*, number 41, October 1987, in **Current Digest of the Soviet Press** (herafter referred to as **CDSP**), volume 39, number 52, 27 January 1988
9. *Pravda*, 2 July 1988, in BBC, **SWB** 0199, 9 July 1988
10. *Izvestia*, 1 February 1987, in **CDSP**, volume 39, number 5, 4 March 1987
11. *Izvestia*, 1 February 1987, in **CDSP**, volume 39, number 5, 4 March 1987
12. *Izvestia*, 1 February 1987, in **CDSP**, volume 39, number 5, 4 March 1987
13. T Mamonova, **Women and Russia: First Feminist Samizdat** (London 1980) pages 5-7

14. Pukhova, in BBC, **SWB**, SU/0199, 9 July 1988
15. Mamonova, page 7
16. Pukhova, in BBC, **SWB**, SU/0199, 9 July 1988
17. Speech by N K Yemelina, director of Smolensk Knitwear Factory, in *Pravda*, 2 July 1988, in BBC, **SWB** 0198, 8 July 1988
18. Mamonova, page 6.
19. *Izvestia*, 1 February 1987, in **CDSP**, volume 39, number 5, 4 March 1987
20. *Izvestia*, 1 February 1987, in **CDSP**, volume 39, number 5, 4 March 1987
21. Mamonova, page 39
22. **Moscow News**, number 40, 1988
23. Pukhova, in BBC, **SWB**, SU/0199, 9 July 1988
24. Heitlinger, page 103
25. Pukhova, in BBC, **SWB**, SU/0199, 9 July 1988
26. Holland, page 12
27. **Moscow News Weekly**, number 44, 1988
28. Mamonova, page 8
29. Mamonova, page xviii
30. Pukhova, in BBC, **SWB**, SU/0199, 9 July 1988

Chapter 2: HOUSING

1. Speech of V I Mironenko, Komsomol First Secretary, to 19th Party Conference, in *Pravda*, 1 July 1988 in BBC, **SWB** 0195, 5 July 1988
2. Minsk TV, 27 July 1988, in BBC, **SWB** 0249, 6 September 1988
3. Mironenko, in BBC, **SWB** 0195, 5 July 1988
4. *Izvestia*, 2 March 1988, in **CDSP**, volume 40, number 9, 30 March 1988
5. S G Arutyunyan, First Secretary Armenian Communist Party Central Committee, on Moscow Home Service, 5 September 1988, in BBC, **SWB** 0253, 10 September 1988
6. **The Guardian**, 11 March 1989
7. *Ogonyok*, number 41, October 1987, in **CDSP**, volume 39, number 52, 27 January 1988
8. Mamonova, page 18
9. *Izvestia*, 10 February 1988, in **CDSP**, volume 10, number 6, 9 March 1988
10. **The Weekend Guardian**, 27-28 May 1989
11. Soviet TV, 14 September 1988, in BBC, **SWB** 0258, 16 Septembr 1988
12. T Cliff, **Russia: A Marxist Analysis** (London 1964) page 295
13. United Nations Compendium of Social Statistics 1977
14. *Pravda*, 24 January 1988, in **CDSP**, volume 40, number 12, 20 April 1988
15. *Argumenty i fakty*, number 32, 1988; Radio Liberty, 17 August 1988
16. United Nations, **Economic Survey of Europe 1949** (Geneva 1950) page 31, in T Cliff, **State Capitalism in Russia** (London 1988) page 54
17. Soviet TV, 14 September 1988, in BBC, **SWB** 0258, 16 September 1988

18. *Pravda*, 1 October 1987, in **CDSP**, volume 39, number 39, 28 October 1987
19. *Pravda*, 1 October 1987, in **CDSP**, volume 39, number 39, 28 October 1987
20. *Pravda*, 27 January 1988, in **CDSP**, volume 40, number 4, 24 February 1988
21. *Izvestia*, 13 March 1988, in **CDSP**, volume 40, number 10, 6 April 1988
22. *Argumenty i fakty*, number 32, 1988
23. *Izvestia*, 13 March 1988, in **CDSP**, volume 40, number 10, 6 April 1988
24. *Izvestia*, 13 March 1988, in **CDSP**, volume 40, number 10, 6 April 1988
25. Soviet TV, 12 September 1988, in BBC, **SWB** 0256, 14 September 1988

Chapter 3: CONSUMER GOODS

1. *Pravda*, 2 July 1988, in BBC, **SWB** 0199, 9 July 1988
2. Holland, page 123
3. Mamonova, page 25
4. *Pravda*, 2 July 1988, in BBC, **SWB** 0197, 7 July 1988
5. **The Economist**, 9 April 1988
6. Mamonova, page 205
7. Moscow Home Service, 21 September 1988, in BBC, **SWB** 0271, 1 October 1988
8. *Pravda*, 20 June 1988, in BBC, **SWB** 0185, 23 June 1988
9. *Pravda*, 23 September 1988, in BBC, **SWB** 0271, 1 October 1988
10. *Pravda ukrainy*, 15 June 1988, in BBC, **SWB** 0185, 23 June 1988
11. **The Economist**, 9 April 1988
12. *Pravda*, 23 Septembr 1988, in BBC, **SWB** 0271, 1 October 1988
13. *Pravda*, 23 Septembr 1988, in BBC, **SWB** 0271, 1 October 1988
14. *Sovetskaya rossia*, quoted in **Financial Times**, 24 December 1988
15. **The Independent**, 18 June 1988
16. **The Guardian**, 17 January 1989
17. **Socialist Worker**, 29 July 1989
18. *Izvestia*, 10 September 1988, in BBC, **SWB** 0044, 23 September 1988
19. *Pravda*, 2 July 1988, in BBC, **SWB** 0197, 7 July 1988
20. Soviet TV, 14 September 1988, in BBC, **SWB** 0258, 16 September 1988
21. *Izvestia*, 10 September 1988, in BBC, **SWB** 0044, 21 September 1988
22. *Izvestia*, 10 September 1988, in BBC, **SWB** 0044, 21 September 1988
23. *Pravda*, 24 January 1988, in **CDSP**, volume 40, number 12, 20 April 1988
24. Quoted in **Financial Times**, 24 December 1988
25. Mamonova, page 25
26. *Komsomolskaya pravda*, 31 January 1987, in **CDSP**, volume 39, number 5, 4 March 1987
27. *Izvestia*, 10 September 1988, in BBC, **SWB** 0044, 23 September 1988; Moscow Home Service, 3 September 1988, in BBC, **SWB** 0255, 13 September 1988

28. **The Economist**, 9 April 1988
29. *Pravda*, 24 January 1988, in **CDSP**, volume 40, number 12, 20 April 1988
30. *Pravda*, 24 January 1988, in **CDSP**, volume 40, number 12, 20 April 1988
31. Moscow Home Service and Soviet TV, 13 September 1988, in BBC, **SWB** 0257, 15 September 1988
32. *Pravda*, December 1987, in **The Economist**, 9 April 1988
33. **MIR**, number 38
34. *Pravda*, 23 September 1988, in BBC, **SWB** 0271, 1 October 1988
35. *Pravda*, 24 January 1988, in **CDSP**, volume 40, number 12, 20 April 1988
36. *Izvestia*, 10 September 1988, in BBC, **SWB** 0044, 23 September 1988
37. *Izvestia*, 10 September 1988, in BBC, **SWB** 0044, 23 September 1988; Moscow Home Service, 3 September 1988, in BBC, **SWB** 0255, 13 September 1988
38. **Financial Times**, 4 December 1988
39. Moscow Home Service, 3 September 1988, in BBC, **SWB** 0255, 13 September 1988
40. *Zvyezda*, 30 August 1988, in BBC, **SWB** 0046, 7 October 1988
41. **Financial Times**, 24 December 1988

Chapter 4: HEALTH

1. *Pravda*, 10 March 1988, in **CDSP**, volume 40, number 10, 6 April 1988
2. *Pravda*, 31 August 1987, in **CDSP**, volume 39, number 35, 30 September 1987
3. Moscow Home Service, 5 September 1988, in BBC, **SWB** 0253, 10 September 1988
4. *Pravda*, 31 August 1987, in **CDSP**, volume 39, number 35, 30 September 1987
5. Moscow Home Service, 12 September 1988, in BBC, **SWB** 0256, 14 September 1988
6. *Pravda*, 30 June 1988, in BBC, **SWB** 0194, 4 July 1988
7. *Pravda*, 30 June 1988, in BBC, **SWB** 0194, 4 July 1988
8. *Pravda*, 30 June 1988, in BBC, **SWB** 0194, 4 July 1988
9. **Weekend Guardian**, 27-28 May 1989
10. **Weekend Guardian**, 27-28 May 1989
11. *Pravda*, 21 July 1988, in **CDSP**, volume 40, number 29, 17 August 1988
12. *Pravda*, 30 June 1988, in BBC, **SWB** 0194, 4 July 1988
13. *Pravda*, 31 August 1987, in **CDSP**, volume 39, number 35, 30 September 1987
14. *Pravda*, 30 June 1988, in BBC, **SWB** 0194, 4 July 1988
15. *Pravda*, 30 June 1988, in BBC, **SWB** 0194, 4 July 1988
16. *Pravda*, 30 June 1988, in BBC, **SWB** 0194, 4 July 1988
17. *Literaturnaya gazeta*, 23 March 1988, in **CDSP**, volume 40, number

14, 4 May 1988

18. *Literaturnaya gazeta*, 23 March 1988, in **CDSP**, volume 40, number 14, 4 May 1988
19. *Pravda*, 30 August 1987, in **CDSP**, volume 39, number 35, 30 September 1987
20. *Pravda*, 31 August 1987, in **CDSP**, volume 39, number 35, 30 September 1987
21. **The Guardian**, 28 Jaunary 1989
22. *Ogonyok*, in **The Independent**, 16 July 1988
23. *Pravda*, 30 June 1988, in BBC, **SWB** 0194, 4 July 1988
24. **The Independent**, 16 July 1988
25. **Financial Times**, 29/30 July 1989
26. Mamonova, page 91
27. **The Independent**, 16 July 1988
28. Scott, page 143
29. Mamonova, page xix
30. BBC 2 Reportage, 22 February 1989
31. *Pravda*, 30 June 1988, in BBC, **SWB** 0194, 4 July 1988
32. *Izvestia*, 2 January 1986, in **CDSP**, volume 38, number 3, 19 February 1986
33. Vitali Vitaliev, in **Weekend Guardian** 27/28 May 1989
34. *Izvestia*, 21 January 1986, in **CDSP**, volume 38, number 3, 19 February 1986; **Financial Times**, 17 January 1989
35. **Moscow News**, in **The Independent**, 30 June 1988

Chapter 5: THE FAMILY

1. *Pravda*, 22 December 1987, in **CDSP**, volume 39, number 51, 20 January 1988
2. Heitlinger, page 84
3. **CDSP**, volume 39, number 52, 27 January 1988
4. Heitlinger, page 84
5. *Chislennost sostav naseleniya SSSR* (Moscow 1984) page 252
6. *Semya*, Radio Liberty, 25 August 1988
7. **Moscow News Weekly**, number 44, 1988
8. Scott, page 143
9. Holland, pages 129-30
10. **The Guardian**, 7 March 1989
11. Mamonova, page 45
12. **MIR**, number 38
13. Holland, page 69
14. Holland, page 70
15. Mamonova, pages 47-8
16. Mamonova, page 91
17. G A Yagodin, Chairman USSR State Committee for Public Education, in *Pravda*, 2 July 1988, in BBC, **SWB** 0198, 8 July 1988

18. Soviet TV, 9 September 1988, in BBC, **SWB** 0259, 17 September 1988
19. *Pravda*, 21 April 1988, in **CDSP**, volume 40, number 16, 18 May 1988
20. *Komsomolskaya Pravda*, 17 December 1987, in **CDSP**, volume 39, number 50, 13 January 1988
21. *Pravda*, 21 April 1988, in **CDSP**, volume 40, number 16, 18 May 1988
22. *Pravda*, 31 August 1987, in **CDSP**, volume 39, number 35, 30 September 1987
23. Mamonova, page 241
24. *Izvestia*, 3 March 1988, in **CDSP**, volume 40, number 9, 30 March 1988
25. *Izvestia*, 3 March 1988, in **CDSP**, volume 40, number 9, 30 March 1988
26. *Sovetskaya pravda*, 5 February 1988
27. *Izvestia*, 3 March 1988, in **CDSP**, volume 40, number 9, 30 March 1988
28. *Izvestia*, 3 March 1988, in **CDSP**, volume 40, number 9, 30 March 1988
29. Tass in Russian for Abroad, 23 July 1988, in BBC, **SWB** 0256, 14 September 1988
30. *Izvestia*, 3 March 1988, in **CDSP**, volume 40, number 9, 30 March 1988
31. Tass in Russian for Abroad, 23 July 1988, in BBC, **SWB** 0256, 14 September 1988
32. *Pravda*, 25 June 1988, in **CDSP**, volume 40, number 25, 20 July 1988
33. Mamonova, page 240
34. Mamonova, pages 18-19
35. 'Uncaptive Minds', September-October 1988
36. Soviet TV, 9 September 1988, in BBC, **SWB** 0259, 17 September 1988

Chapter 6: PROSTITUTION

1. *Sovetskaya rossia*, 12 March 1987, in **CDSP**, volume 39, number 11, 15 April 1987
2. *Sovetskaya belorussia*, 10 May 1987, in **CDSP**, volume 39, number 42, 18 November 1987
3. *Trud*, 76 February 1988, in **CDSP**, volume 40, number 8, 23 March 1988
4. **CDSP**, volume 39, number 42, 18 November 1987
5. **CDSP**, volume 39, number 42, 18 November 1987
6. *Sovetskaya belorussia*, 6 December 1987, in **CDSP**, volume 39, number 50, 13 January 1988
7. *Komsomolskaya pravda*, 9 October 1986, in **CDSP**, volume 38, number 41, 12 November 1986
8. *Komsomolskaya pravda*, 19 September 1987, in **CDSP**, volume 39, number 42, 18 November 1987
9. *Sovetskaya rossia*, 19 March 1987, in **CDSP**, volume 39, number 11, 15 April 1987
10. *Sovetskaya belorussia*, 13 November 1987, in **CDSP**, volume 40, number 8, 23 March 1988
11. *Sovetskaya rossia*, 19 March 1987, in **CDSP**, volume 39, number 11, 15 April 1987
12. *Sovetskaya rossia*, 12 March 1987; *Nedelya*, number 21, 1987

13. *Sovetskaya rossia*, 12 March 1987, in **CDSP**, volume 39, number 11, 15 April 1987

14. *Nedelya*, number 12, 1987, in **CDSP**, volume 39, number 11, 15 April 1987

15. *Trud*, 31 July 1987, in **CDSP**, volume 40, number 8, 23 March 1988

16. *Sotsiologicheskiye issledovania*, number 6, November-December 1987, in **CDSP**, volume 40, number 8, 23 March 1988

17. *Sovetskaya rossia*, 12 March 1987, in **CDSP**, volume 39, number 11, 15 April 1987

18. *Sovetskaya rossia*, 12 March 1987, in **CDSP**, volume 39, number 11, 15 April 1987

19. *Sotsiologicheskiye issledovania*, number 6, November-December 1987, in **CDSP**, volume 40, number 8, 23 March 1988

20. *Pravda ukrainy*, 29 March 1987, in **CDSP**, volume 39, number 42, 18 November 1987

21. *Sotsiologicheskiye issledovania*, number 6, November-December 1987, in **CDSP**, volume 40, number 8, 23 March 1988

22. *Sotsiologicheskiye issledovania*, number 6, November-December 1987, in **CDSP**, volume 40, number 8, 23 March 1988

23. *Pravda*, 3 February 1988, in **CDSP**, volume 40, number 5, 2 March 1988

24. *Literaturnaya gazeta*, 16 September 1987, in **CDSP**, volume 39, number 42, 18 November, 1987

25. *Zarya vostoka*, 25 September 1987, in **CDSP**, volume 39, number 42, 16 November 1987

26. *Sovetskaya rossia*, 19 March 1987, in **CDSP**, volume 39, number 11, 15 April 1987

27. *Trud*, 21 July 1987, in **CDSP**, volume 40, number 8, 23 March 1988

28. *Komsomolskaya pravda*, 19 September 1987, in **CDSP**, volume 39, number 42, 18 November 1987

29. *Pravda ukrainy*, 29 March 1987, in **CDSP**, volume 39, number 42, 18 November 1987

30. *Komsomolskaya pravda*, 17 December 1987, in **CDSP**, volume 39, number 50, 13 January 1988

31. *Komsomolskaya pravda*, 17 December 1987, in **CDSP**, volume 39, number 50, 13 January 1988

32. *Sovetskaya belorussia*, 6 December 1987, in **CDSP**, volume 39, number 50, 13 January 1988

33. Mamonova, page 20

34. *Pravda*, 26 June 1988, in **CDSP**, volume 40, number 26, 27 July 1988

PART TWO: 1917 AND WOMEN'S EMANCIPATION
Chapter 1: WOMEN UNDER TSARISM

1. Quoted in T Cliff, **Class Struggle and Women's Liberation** (London 1984) page 91

2. S A Smith, **Red Petrograd: Revolution in the Factories 1917-18**

(Cambridge 1983) page 12

3. Smith, page 25
4. R L Glickman, **Russian Factory Women: Workplace and Society 1880-1914** (London 1984) page 23
5. Smith, page 29
6. Smith, page 9
7. Smith, page 10
8. Smith, page 23
9. Smith, pages 24-5
10. Glickman, pages 11-14
11. Smith, page 14
12. F Blekher, **The Soviet Woman in the Family and in Society** (Jerusalem 1979) page 10
13. Smith, page 48
14. Glickman, pages 67-8
15. Glickman, page 143
16. Blekher, page 10
17. Glickman, page 63
18. Glickman, page 67
19. Smith, page 42
20. Blekher, page 10
21. Glickman, page 61
22. Glickman, page 145
23. Glickman, pages 33-4
24. Glickman, page 203
25. Glickman, page 111; Smith, page 34
26. Glickman, pages 162-3
27. T Cliff, **Lenin: Building the Party** (London 1975) page 58
28. Cliff, **Class Struggle and Women's Liberation**, page 92
29. Glickman, page 217
30. Glickman, page 205
31. Glickman, page 212
32. Quoted in Cliff, **Class Struggle and Women's Liberation**, page 100

Chapter 2: LIBERATION THROUGH REVOLUTION

1. Quoted in Cliff, **Class Struggle and Women's Liberation**, pages 105-6
2. Quoted in Cliff, **Class Struggle and Women's Liberation**, page 106
3. L Trotsky, **History of the Russian Revolution** (London 1934) page 122
4. Trotsky, **History of the Russian Revolution**, pages 108-9
5. Quoted in Cliff, **Class Struggle and Women's Liberation**, page 107
6. Smith, page 193
7. Smith, pages 67-8
8. Smith, page 160

9. Smith, page 111
10. Smith, page 114
11. Smith, page 72
12. Smith, page 193
13. Cliff, **Class Struggle and Women's Liberation**, page 108
14. Smith, page 194
15. Smith, pages 98-100
16. Smith, page 194
17. Cliff, **Class Struggle and Women's Liberation**, pages 107-8
18. Smith, page 195
19. Smith, page 195
20. Smith, page 175
21. Smith, page 176
22. I Deutscher (editor) **The Age of Permanent Revolution: A Trotsky Anthology** (New York 1964) page 301
23. V I Lenin, Speech at First All-Russian Congress of Working Women, 16 November 1918
24. V Bilshai, **The Status of Women in the Soviet Union** (Moscow 1957) page 23
25. Tolkunova, *Pravo zhenshchinna trud: ego garantii* (Moscow 1967) page 124
26. **International Labour Review**, October 1929, in Cliff, **State Capitalism in Russia**, page 39
27. K Zetkin, **Reminiscences of Lenin** (London 1929)
28. Cliff, **Class Struggle and Women's Liberation**, page 140
29. Blekher, page 10
30. Heitlinger, **Women and State Socialism**, page 59
31. Bilshai, page 42
32. Bilshai, page 42
33. Cliff, **Class Struggle and Women's Liberation**, page 145
34. Deutscher (editor), page 300
35. C Rosenberg, **Education and Revolution: A Great Experiment in Socialist Education** (London no date) page 4
36. Cliff, **Class Struggle and Women's Liberation**, page 146-7
37. R Stites, **The Women's Liberation Movement in Russia** (Princetown 1978) page 372
38. S M Schwarz, **Labor in the Soviet Union** (New York 1952) page 65

Chapter 3: STALINISM

1. T Cliff, **Lenin: Revolution Besieged** (London 1987) page 208
2. Cliff, **Lenin: Revolution Besieged**, page 208
3. Cliff, **Class Struggle and Women's Liberation**, page 146
4. J Stalin, 'Problems of Leninism', in I Deutscher, **Stalin**, (Oxford University Press 1949) page 32
5. P Binns, T Cliff and C Harman, **Russia: From Workers' State to State**

Capitalism (London 1987) page 48
6. Holland, pages 38-9
7. Schwarz, page 288
8. Schwarz, page 72
9. Schwarz, pages 74-5
10. *Trud*, in Schwarz, page 289
11. *Trud*, in Schwarz, page 289
12. Schwarz, pages 98-102
13. *Sovetskaya yustitsia*, number 22, 1940, page 3, in Schwarz, page 114
14. W W Kulski, **The Soviet Regime: Communism in Practice** (Syracuse University Press 1954) page 344
15. Schwarz, page 389
16. Schwarz, page 134
17. Schwarz, page 262
18. Schwarz, page 285
19. Schwarz, page 165
20. Kulski, page 415
21. V I Lenin, **Works** (in Russian), volume xxvii, page 132
22. Schwarz, pages 148-9
23. A Biryukova, **The Working Woman in the USSR** (Moscow 1973) page 14
24. Pinkevich, **Education in the USSR**, quoted in Rosenberg, page 15
25. Kulski, page 511
26. Kulski, page 415
27. Zetkin, page 69
28. G N Serebrennikov, **The Position of Women in the USSR** (London 1937) page 147
29. Schwarz, page 308
30. *Voprosy truda*, May-June 1931, in Schwarz, page 310
31. Schwarz, page 317
32. A S Makarenko, quoted in Kulski, page 496
33. K Millett, **Sexual Politics** (London 1977) page 174
34. L Trotsky, **The Revolution Betrayed** (New York 1972) page 153
35. Sadvokasova, *Sotsial'no gigiencheskie aspekty regulirovaniya a razmerov sem'i* (Moscow 1969) page 125, in J Evans, 'Women and Family Policy in the USSR 1936-1941' (PhD thesis, University of Birmingham 1987) page 232
36. E Klenitskaya and L Melnikova, *Rabota akusherkina sele* (Alma Ata 1954) page 27, in Evans, page 196
37. *Trud*, 27 April 1937, in Evans, page 26
38. *Izvestia*, 28 June 1937, in Evans, page 196
39. Sadvokasova, pages 29-30 and 116, in Evans, page 205
40. *Rabotnitsa*, number 17, 1938, in Evans, page 188; *Izvestia*, 27 June 1938, in Evans, page 188.
41. *Sotsialisticheskaya zakonnost*, number 8, 1937, in Evans, page 197

42. K Mehnert, **The Anatomy of Soviet Man** (London 1961) page 51; Cliff, **Class Struggle and Women's Liberation**, pages 150-1

43. Cliff,**Class Struggle and Women's Liberation**, page 151

44. Trotsky, **Revolution Betrayed**, page 188

45. Trotsky, **Revolution Betrayed**, page 145

Chapter 6: WHAT DOES PERESTROIKA OFFER?

1. **The Economist**, 9 April 1988
2. Letter to *Pravda*, 20 June 1988, in BBC, **SWB** 0185, 23 June 1988
3. Moscow Home Service, 13 September 1988, in BBC, **SWB**, 0257, 15 September 1988
4. **The Economist**, 9 April 1988
5. *Pravda*, 23 September 1988, in BBC, **SWB** 0271, 1 October 1988
6. *Pravda*, 1 July 1988, in BBC, **SWB** 0196, 6 July 1988
7. *Pravda*, 23 September 1988, in BBC, **SWB** 0271, 1 October 1988
8. **The Guardian**, 17 June 1989
9. *Izvestia*, 6 May 1988, in BBC, **SWB** 0148, 11 May 1988
10. Soviet TV, 12 September 1988, in BBC, **SWB** 0256, 14 September 1988
11. **MIR**, number 38
12. Pukhova, in BBC, **SWB**, SU/0199, 9 July 1988.
13. *Pravda*, 25 June 1988, in **CDSP**, volume 40, number 25, 20 July 1988
14. *Pravda*, 20 March 1987, in **CDSP**, volume 39, number 12, 22 April 1987
15. *Noorte Haal* (in Estonian) 19 August 1988, in BBC, **SWB** 0253, 10 September 1988
16. *Pravda*, 20 March 1987, in **CDSP** volume 39, number 12, 22 April 1987; *Pravda*, 24 January 1987, in **CDSP**, volume 40, number 12, 20 April 1988
17. *Izvestia*, 2 March 11988, in **CDSP** volume 40, number 9, 30 March 1988
18. *Pravda*, 2 July 1988, in BBC, **SWB** 0199, 9 July 1988
19. Moscow Home Service, 14 September 1988, in BBC, **SWB** 0258, 16 September 1988
20. **Socialist Worker**, 29 July 1989
21. Pukhova, in BBC, **SWB**, SU/0199, 9 July 1988
22. Pukhova, in BBC, **SWB**, SU/0199, 9 July 1988
23. Tass, 26 May 1988, in BBC, **SWB** 0163, 28 May 1988
24. *Zarya vostoka*, 12 July 1988, in BBC, **SWB** 0253, 10 September 1988
25. Tass in English, 31 August 1988, in BBC, **SWB** 0253, 10 September 1988
26. *Pravda*, 12 June 1988, in **CDSP**, volume 40, number 24, 13 July 1988
27. Reuters-Associated Press, 9 September 11988
28. Yerevan in Armenian for Europe, 11 July 1988, in BBC, **SWB** 0202, 13 July 1988
29. Tass in English, 23 June 1988, in BBC, **SWB** 0191, 30 June 1988
30. *Izvestia*, 15 March 1988, in **CDSP** 40, 10, 6 April 1988
31. Moscow Home Service, 30 June 1988, in BBC, **SWB** 0194, 4 July 1988
32. *Pravda*, 11 May 1988, in BBC, **SWB** 0181, 18 June 1988

33. Soviet TV, 13 June 1988, in BBC, **SWB** 0181, 18 June 1988
34. *Izvestia*, 21 July 1988, in **CDSP** volume 40, number 29, 1988
35. Soviet TV, 13 June 1988, in BBC, **SWB** 0181, 18 June 1988
36. Soviet TV, 14 June 1988, in BBC, **SWB** 0183, 21 June 1988
37. *Pravda*, 11 May 1988, in BBC, **SWB** 0150, 13 May 1988
38. *Pravda*, 1 July 1988, in BBC, **SWB** 0197, 7 July 1988
39. Soviet TV, 12 September 1988, in BBC, **SWB** 0256, 14 September 1988
40. Soviet TV, 13 September 1988, in BBC, **SWB** 0258, 16 September 1988
41. *Izvestia*, no date, in BBC, **SWB** 0250, 7 September 1988
42. *Izvestia*, 15 March 1988, in **CDSP**, volume 40, number 10, 6 April 1988

Index

Abortion: 44, 45, 79, 94, 95
Aganbegyan A: 21, 107
Aids: 43, 44
Alienation: 9, 98, 110
Armenia: 22, 25
Azerbaijan: 22, 105

Barter: 32
Belorussia: 21, 56
Beauty contest: 62
Birthrate: 48, 94, 96, 97, 101
'Black Saturdays': 19
Bolsheviks: 72-4, 76, 79, 81, 82, 84, 111
—and equal pay: 78
—and the family: 101
Brazil: 10, 31
Brezhnev L: 11, 105
Bride price: 52
Buckley M: 7

Chazov Y I: 39-41, 45
Child care: 92, 111
Clothing: 33, 34
Committee of Soviet Women: 20, 102
Communist Party: 20, 26, 27, 36, 41
Consumer goods, and consumption: 9, 28, 30, 31, 86, 93, 97-8, 99, 111

Contraceptives: 44, 79, 94
Co-operatives: 35, 45, 46, 98
Corruption: 9, 36, 41, 104, 106
Cotton-growing: 43
Creches: 92

Discriminatory pay: 9
Divorce: 9, 47, 82, 94, 101
—and prostitution: 59
Domestic appliances: 34
Dormitories: 16, 22, 23, 24
Drunkenness: 9, 47, 52-3, 60

Education: 15, 20, 59
Egalitarianism, 'levelling out': 76, 90, 92, 106
Eight-hour day: 76, 79
Equal pay: 15, 78, 79, 90
Estonia: 21, 22, 101, 102

Factory committees: 96-7
Family: 9, 47-55, 93, 94, 100-1, 111
—in the October revolution: 80
Feminists: 7, 54
Fines: 70
Five Year Plans: 10, 18, 19, 28, 34, 38, 86, 89, 90, 91, 109
Food poisoning: 9, 41
Fruit and vegetable supply, in Moscow: 32, 33

Georgia: 56
Glasnost: 9, 11, 35, 56, 96, 98, 100, 104, 105
Gorbachev M S: 9, 24, 25, 33, 34, 35, 39, 97, 98, 99, 102, 104, 106, 109, 110, 111
—and anti-alcohol campaign: 53
—on egalitarianism: 90
—on the family: 100
—on housing: 21
—promotes co-operatives: 45

Health: 38-46
Homelessness: 9, 24
Hospitals: 9, 38, 39, 45, 104
Housing: 21-9, 104, 111
—under Tsarism: 69
—in Britain: 28

India: 10, 30
Industrial revolution: 10
Infanticide: 95
Infant mortality: 41, 70
Institute for Protection of Mothers and Children: 42
International Women's Day: 74-5, 87
1905 revolution: 72
19th Party Conference: 40, 102

Kazakhstan: 40
Khrushchev N S: 11, 26, 99, 100
Kindergartens: 26, 28, 92, 102, 104, 105
Kirghizstan: 27, 56
Kollontai A: 67, 80

Labour
—Code: 80, 88
—division of: 15
—heavy: 79-80
—legislation: 79
Latvia: 22
Lenin V I: 7, 79, 80, 81, 84, 93

—on 'levelling out': 90-1
'Levelling out'
—see Egalitarianism
Limitchiki: 16, 20, 22
Lithuania: 37
'Living torches': 52, 55

Mamonova T: 45
Marx K: 7, 8, 67, 77, 86, 87, 93
Maternity benefits: 19, 93
Maternity hospitals: 39, 45, 80
Moscow: 16, 20, 22, 23, 25, 27, 40, 50, 81, 82
—bread riots in 1905: 74
—child care centres: 49
—communal feeding after revolution: 80
—divorce: 47
—fruit and vegetable provision: 32, 95
—homes for abandoned children: 48
—liquor shops: 53
—1980 Olympics: 61
—prostitution: 56, 57, 58
Motherhood: 8, 10, 95
—'Heroine Mothers': 19, 28
—single mothers: 59
Multi-shift working: 19

'N-products': 37
'National interest': 9
New Economic Policy (NEP): 56, 82, 85
Night work: 18, 80, 82, 89
Nurseries: 9, 19, 80, 82

October revolution: 10, 56, 63, 78, 79, 90, 91, 93
Overtime: 19

Part-time working: 15, 102
Perestroika: 9, 11, 54, 96, 98, 99, 101, 103-9, 111

Piecework: 91
Pollution: 9
Prostitution: 9, 56-62, 81, 83, 95
—in Belorussia: 57
—'foreign specialists': 57-8
—under Tsarism: 69, 71
Protective legislation: 79, 88, 90
—Britain and Russia compared: 17
Pukhova Z P: 16, 31, 102

Rape: 61
Rationing: 33, 99
Religion: 54-5, 103
—Islam: 54-5
—in the Ukraine: 54
RSFSR: 22, 57

Samizdat: 24
'Sanitary norm': 26
Schools: 9, 49, 50, 82
Scott H: 7
Servants: 70
Sex: 44, 47, 49, 81, 93
Sexual harassment: 70
'Shearers': 61
Shiftwork: 89
Stakhanovism: 91
Stalin J V: 10, 18, 24, 44, 63, 85,
86, 87, 90, 93, 94, 106, 111
—on abortion: 94
—on overtaking the West: 21
Stalinism: 84-95
State capitalism: 8, 11, 63, 86, 95,
97, 106, 111
Strikes
—miners': 33, 102
—over equal pay: 78
—under Tsarism: 71, 72

Tajikistan: 22
—population increase: 48

—'living torches': 52
Tereshkova V V: 19
Textile industry: 67, 76
Textile workers: 15, 68-9, 71, 73,
74, 75
Tobacco-growing: 41-3
Trade unions: 77, 91-2
—lack of help for women: 16
—membership: 81
—and protective legislation: 17
Transport: 9, 30, 31, 47
Trotsky L D: 7, 79, 82, 95, 111
—and Left Opposition: 85
—on the family: 94
Turkmenia: 28, 41, 105
—arranged marriages: 52
—Institute for Protecting the
Health of Mother and Child: 38-9
—melon production: 43

Ukraine: 56, 87
Unemployment: 82, 85, 111
Uzbekistan: 48, 50

Venereal disease (VD): 60, 83
Vitaliev V: 25, 40

Wage differentials: 15, 76, 90, 91
'Woman question': 11, 95
Women and Russia: 31, 45, 49,
53, 62
Women's liberation: 7, 10, 63, 80,
82, 83, 84, 87, 95
Women workers
—conditions for: 17
—heavy labour: 17, 18
—in the mines: 87
—percentage of working class: 15

Zhenotdel: 81, 87
Zetkin K: 92

Other titles published by Bookmarks

include

Sex, Class and Socialism / *Lindsey German*
An examination of the relationship between women and work, the family
and women's oppression. £5.95 / US$10.00

Class Struggle and Women's Liberation / *Tony Cliff*
A history of the struggle for women's liberation, from the 16th century to
today, in Britain, the US, Russia, France and Germany. £4.95 / US$9.75

Women's Liberation and Socialism / *Celia Petty, Deborah Roberts and
Sharon Smith*
An account of the role played by socialists in the fight for women's
liberation, and the relationship between the two struggles. £1.95 / US$3.75

Rosa Luxemburg / *Tony Cliff*
A political biography of one of the most revolutionary thinkers of our
century. £2.50 / $4.75

Available through bookshops everywhere.
If you have difficulty obtaining Bookmarks publications, we run mail order
services from London, Chicago and Melbourne and will send books
anywhere in the world. Our London bookshop stocks books and pamphlets
from many publishers on socialism, internationalism, trade union struggle,
women's issues, the Marxist classics, economics and much more.
Write for our latest booklists to:

BOOKMARKS

265 Seven Sisters Road, Finsbury Park, London N4 2DE, England
PO Box 16085, Chicago, IL 60616, USA
GPO Box 1473N, Melbourne 3001, Australia